WEST ACADEMIC PUBLISHING'S EMERITUS ADVISORY BOARD

JESSE H. CHOPER
Professor of Law and Dean Emeritus
University of California, Berkeley

LARRY D. KRAMER
President and Vice Chancellor and Professor of Law
The London School of Economics and Political Science

GRANT S. NELSON
Professor of Law Emeritus, Pepperdine University
Professor of Law Emeritus, University of California, Los Angeles

JAMES J. WHITE
Robert A. Sullivan Emeritus Professor of Law
University of Michigan

AF869598

WEST ACADEMIC PUBLISHING'S LAW SCHOOL ADVISORY BOARD

MARK C. ALEXANDER
Arthur J. Kania Dean and Professor of Law
Villanova University Charles Widger School of Law

JOSHUA DRESSLER
Distinguished University Professor Emeritus
Michael E. Moritz College of Law, The Ohio State University

MEREDITH J. DUNCAN
Alumnae College Professor of Law
Assistant Dean for Strategic Opportunities, Pedagogy, and Faculty, Student, and Community Engagement, University of Houston Law Center

RENEE KNAKE JEFFERSON
Joanne and Larry Doherty Chair in Legal Ethics and Professor of Law, University of Houston Law Center

ORIN S. KERR
Professor of Law
Stanford Law School

RENÉE HUTCHINS LAURENT
Dean & Professor of Law
University of Maryland Carey School of Law

JONATHAN R. MACEY
Professor of Law
Yale Law School

DEBORAH JONES MERRITT
Distinguished University Professor
John Deaver Drinko/Baker & Hostetler Chair in Law Emerita
Michael E. Moritz College of Law, The Ohio State University

ARTHUR R. MILLER
University Professor and Chief Justice Warren E. Burger Professor of Constitutional Law and the Courts, New York University

A. BENJAMIN SPENCER
Dean & Trustee Professor of Law
William & Mary Law School

CALIFORNIA BABY BAR SUCCESS

A Comprehensive Guide

Second Edition

Sara J. Berman
Professor of Lawyering Skills and Director of the Academic Success Program,
University of Southern California Gould School of Law

WEST ACADEMIC

The publisher is not engaged in rendering legal or other professional advice, and this publication is not a substitute for the advice of an attorney. If you require legal or other expert advice, you should seek the services of a competent attorney or other professional.

© 2023 LEG, Inc. d/b/a West Academic
© 2026 LEG, Inc. d/b/a West Academic
860 Blue Gentian Road, Suite 350
Eagan, MN 55121
1-877-888-1330

West, West Academic Publishing, and West Academic are trademarks of West Publishing Corporation, used under license.

Published in the United States of America

ISBN: 979-8-89545-608-8

To all of my students who have gone on to be great lawyers.

ACKNOWLEDGMENTS

Profound gratitude to Pamela Siege Chandler, Louis Higgins, John Moen, Megan Putler and everyone at West, with special thanks to the production team including Laura Holle, Megan Hoffman, Whitney Esson, Bridget Davis, and Michele Bassett.

INTRODUCTION

Let's start with this: the *First-Year Law Students' Examination (FYLSE or FYLSX),* and *"baby bar"* are synonyms and will be used interchangeably throughout this book.

In the words of the bar examiners:

The First-Year Law Students' Examination, or "baby bar," is administered in June and October. The exam is comprised of 100 multiple-choice questions. Two exam sessions are available each day, allowing applicants to choose between a morning or afternoon session. There is one set break in each session.

If you are an enrolled student or will begin your legal education at a law school in California that is not accredited by the American Bar Association or California State Bar, or if you are participating in California's Law Office Study Program, or if you must take the California Baby Bar for another reason, this book is for you. The book provides some basics about exam strategies that will help on both law school exams and the Baby Bar.

Remember: you may **not** need to take this exam. Only certain students need to take it. Please study https://www.calbar.ca.gov/Admissions/Examinations/First-Year-Law-Students-Examination to determine whether you must take the first year law student's exam and to understand the exam policies and procedures.

As noted on the State Bar website:

Not all law students have to take the baby bar. Law students completing their first year of law study in a juris doctor degree program at a State Bar-unaccredited registered law school, or through the Law Office Study Program, and those without two years of college work attending a California-accredited or an American Bar Association (ABA)-accredited law school must take the

First-Year Law Students' Exam after completing their first year of law study.

Law students who have advanced to their second year of law study at an ABA or California-accredited law school and who have completed a minimum of 60 semester, or 90 quarter units of undergraduate work are generally exempt from the exam.

[https://www.calbar.ca.gov/Admissions/Examinations/First-Year-Law-Students-Examination]

This book is a success strategy guide; it is not a rule book. All the rules you need for the Baby Bar are in **West's *Step-by-Step Guides* to Torts, Contracts, and Criminal Law**.

Step-by-Step Guide to Torts

- Sara J. Berman & Steven J. Bracci
- 1st edition, ©2022

Step-by-Step Guide to Contracts

- Sara J. Berman & Steven J. Bracci
- 1st edition, ©2022

Step-by-Step Guide to Criminal Law

- Sara J. Berman & Steven J. Bracci
- 1st edition, ©2022

And, you will find all the practice multiple choice questions you need in the **Adaptibar** FYLSX course.

With this book, the *Step-by-Step Guides*, and Adaptibar, you have all the resources you need. These also provide motivation to study, strategies to overcome challenges, and techniques to help you achieve your success goals.

Depending on when you are reading this book, that goal may be to pass the Baby Bar the first time around, or the next time (if you are repeating the exam).

THIS BOOK IS FOR LAW STUDENTS
AND THEIR FAMILIES & FRIENDS

If you are in law school and getting ready to take California's Baby Bar, this book is *written for you and to you.* This book will provide training tips to get you ready for success; it will push you to do your very best. This book will also help families, friends, spouses, and partners understand just how stressful and time consuming the exam really is. It is not, "just another test."

Let's also get something straight: despite common terminology which we use here because it's what everyone calls the exam, the FYLSX is *not* a *baby* anything. It is a difficult exam and you need to do a lot of work to pass. The sooner you understand the rules of this game, the easier it will be.

YOU CAN PASS!

There are many who will tell you that you cannot pass this test, that the odds are against you. But you can. Read on and learn what steps to take. Believe you can, set your goals, and work hard.

What if you think, *"Well, I am no good at standardized tests. I did lousy on the SAT, and I am surely not going to pass the FYLSX first time around. I know so many smart classmates who failed. Why am I different?"* In part my answer is, "You are different because you are reading this book."

The rest of my answer is this, put yourself in charge with a growth mindset—a firm conviction that your abilities *can* develop and improve.

A fixed mindset says, "I did poorly in 1L, so I'm no good at law school." Or, "I got a bad grade in contracts, so I'm never going to understand contracts." By contrast, a *growth* mindset says, "I'm going to figure out what I can do differently and study as hard as possible so that my understanding continuously improves until I have a strong command of contracts, torts, and criminal law."

A growth mindset allows you to enjoy studying because every "mistake" is simply an opportunity to learn!

IS THE BABY BAR THAT BAD?

It's a hard test. It's exhausting. It's a lot of material to learn in three key subjects, torts, contracts, and criminal law. Classmates may share their horror stories. But studying for the FYLSX does not have to be "torture." You can view it that way and be miserable for months. Or you can embrace it as an opportunity to master three heavily tested and critically important subjects and a variety of lawyering skills. Call it a down payment for success on the Bar Exam!

Bottom line: if passing this exam is something you must do to become a licensed California attorney, look at its bright sides—including finding ways to thrive in the face of challenge, guiding you to a lifetime of success.

> FACT PATTERNS AS PUZZLES
>
> MCQ exam fact patterns will be fun to resolve when you have mastered criminal law, torts, and contracts, using West's *Step-by-Step Guides*. Think about how *not fun* it would be to do a crossword puzzle in a language you don't understand. By the time you take the Baby Bar, you should be able to honestly say, *"Bring it on! Throw any fact pattern at me. I may not remember every detail of every rule, but I know enough to rule out some wrong answers and reason to the best answer because of the dedicated time and effort I've put into studying and taking practice exams, and because of the reasoning skills I have developed. I will carefully read the facts they give me, think logically, and do this. I am ready."*

If you are working while in school, or if you have extensive family responsibilities, the juggling may be the hardest part.

You may be the first in your family to attend college or law school. You may face "impostor syndrome," and the mistaken, but natural, understandable, and very common feeling that you don't belong. You *do belong*.

A primary mission of this book is to change attitudes along with study approaches—to give FYLSX applicants, no matter your *statistical* chance of passing, the tools *and* confidence to break free of fixed mindsets that tell you that you can't.

But let me be very clear: this book is *not* about magic, bestowing false confidence, or hollow pep talks. It is about the determined and grounded belief that if you work hard and sensibly, and remain doggedly motivated, you can trust that you will succeed.

So, whether you are just starting law school or have finished your first year, if the FYLSX is a gate you must jump, then consider it the big event. You will need to give it your all, just as you would if you were starring in a Broadway show or climbing an enormous mountain peak.

Do not dread this process. But do not underestimate how much it will take. Climbing this mountain will be tough. Use every last ounce of energy. Don't hold back. Learning to commit with total focus and use resources and strategies for success on this exam will help you do well in law school, pass the bar exam after graduation, and enjoy your future legal career.

"Always bear in mind that your own resolution to succeed is more important than any other thing."

—ABRAHAM LINCOLN—

ABOUT THE AUTHOR

Sara J. Berman has served as a law professor and director of academic and bar success programs in law schools in California, NY, and Florida, and lectured in bar reviews for more than two decades, helping thousands of students pass law school exams, the baby bar, and bar exams nationwide.

West Publications by Sara J. Berman

1L Success: Becoming a Lawyer, a Professional Identity Formation Workbook

- Sara J. Berman
- 1st edition, ©2024
- (2d ed. forthcoming, 2026)

Bar Exam Success: A Comprehensive Guide

- Sara J. Berman
- 2nd edition, ©2023
- (3d ed. forthcoming, 2026)

2L Success: Lawyering Skills Training & Professional Identity Formation for Upper Division Law Students

- Sara J. Berman
- 1st edition, ©2025

Bar Exam Prep for the Next Generation: Building a Solid Foundation Before Bar Review Begins

- Steven I. Friedland & Sara J. Berman
- 1st edition, ©2025

Bar Exam MPT Preparation & Experiential Learning for Law Students

- Sara J. Berman
- 2nd edition, ©2021
- (3d ed. forthcoming, as **Performance Test Success: Bar Preparation and Experiential Learning Simulations for Law Students**, 2025)

Office Hours on Academic Success (Audio)

- Sara J. Berman
- Set 1 ©2022
- Set 2 ©2023

Office Hours on Bar Exam Success (Audio)

- Sara J. Berman
- ©2023

Step-by-Step Guide to Torts

- Sara J. Berman & Steven J. Bracci
- 1st edition, ©2022
- 2d ed. anticipated 2025

Step-by-Step Guide to Contracts

- Sara J. Berman & Steven J. Bracci
- 1st edition, ©2022
- 2d ed. anticipated 2025

Step-by-Step Guide to Criminal Law

- Sara J. Berman & Steven J. Bracci
- 1st edition, ©2022
- 2d ed. anticipated 2025

TABLE OF CONTENTS

CALIFORNIA BABY BAR SUCCESS

A Comprehensive Guide

Second Edition

CHAPTER 1

SET YOUR GOAL AND COMMIT TO SUCCESS

CHAPTER SUMMARY: In this Chapter, you will begin preparing for success by setting your intention and breaking free from doubts that may prevent your success.

The FYLSX is a *tough, high stakes exams.* We call it the Baby Bar, but don't let that fool you. It's 100 tricky multiple choice questions. A lot rides on passing it. Many students fail and, sadly, many *expect* to fail. Not you. Ban thoughts such as, "I can take it again if need be." No. From now on, do what it takes to succeed.

Demystify the exam:

- Master Torts, Contracts, and Criminal Law with West's *Step-by-Step Guides* to each of those subjects.
- Enroll in and complete the multiple choice practice in Adaptibar's FYLSX course. And,
- Carefully study the information on the California Bar's website at https://www.calbar.ca.gov/Admissions/Examinations/First-Year-Law-Students-Examination.

Also avoid the trap of false confidence and *assuming* the FYLSX can't be that hard. (After all, you already studied these subjects in law school.) No. It *is* that hard.

You *can* pass this exam, but *only* if you work really hard, understand what it takes, commit to success, and plan ahead.

Note: This is not: "I will because I always succeed" or "I will because I deserve to." ***This is:*** "I will because I am determined to do what it takes to pass, no matter how difficult and time consuming."

Take a moment and closely watch some really successful people. Most work very hard at what they do. And, you would not have gone to law school in the first place if you weren't a person who thrived on challenge. So, please do not go into this Baby Bar process thinking you will merely "give it a shot" and see how it goes. Invest in success, train for success, and see that you achieve it.

"I will PASS the 20___ Baby Bar!"

Name: ______________________ Date: ________

Signature: ____________________ Date: ________

Self-Assessment: Find Your "Why"

What will passing the Baby Bar mean for you?

____

____

____

Why do you want to be a lawyer?

____

____

____

USE POSITIVE SELF-TALK

Think of yourself *and speak of yourself* as someone who can *and will* succeed. Consider the following examples:

- *Self-Talk*: Why do I keep scoring so low on practice tests?
- ***Rephrase***: How can I improve my practice scores? Making mistakes with practice tests is the best way to learn. The more I learn, the better my score will be on the actual exam.

- *Self-Talk*: Contracts is confusing. I'll *never* understand it.
- ***Rephrase***: Maybe I need to reread explanations or find different explanations, but I will get it eventually.
- *Self-Talk*: I'll never be able to sit and focus for that many multiple choice questions in a row.
- ***Rephrase***: It will be challenging to build the endurance I need. I will have to train, increasing my study time each day so that I'm ready to perform when I must be *on* and focused for my FYLSX.
- *Self-Talk*: I have crazy test anxiety. I cannot confidently say I will pass this FYLSX.
- ***Rephrase***: I acknowledge legitimate fear, but I won't let it block me. I will leverage my anxiety as adrenaline. I will turn "*panic* into *power* not *paralysis*." Fear can become the most powerful of motivators. It can make you stronger and more prepared for success.

What doubts do you need to rephrase?

- *Self-Talk*: ______________________________

  ____
- ***Rephrase***: ______________________________

  ____
- *Self-Talk*: ______________________________

  ____
- ***Rephrase***: ______________________________

  ____

Imagine It Is Three Weeks Before Your FYLSX

How will you describe your feelings about the exam? Choose one:

A. I'm dying here!

B. I am taking this exam and hoping like hell that I pass.

C. This is the worst; knowing my luck, I'll be taking it again.

D. I'm training for success on this exam. The experience is giving me an opportunity to review and solidify all the learning I have done in contracts, torts, and criminal law—subjects that I will still have to know well after graduation to pass the bar exam. I'm becoming a stronger and more skilled reader and thinker. I will do this. I will pass the Baby Bar.

The right answer is D!

"We gain strength, and courage, and confidence by each experience in which we really stop to look fear in the face . . . we must do that which we think we cannot."

—ELEANOR ROOSEVELT—

TOP TEN BABY BAR SUCCESS TIPS

1. Decide to pass.

Think positively. Do not tell yourself, "I can always take it again."

2. Align your priorities with your decision to pass.

Make your priorities studying, sleeping, eating right, and exercising.

3. You study with reliable materials.

Use reliable content to study from, such as West's *Step-by-Step Guides* to Criminal Law, Contracts, and Torts, and Adaptibar.

4. You keep your study schedule.

Calendar what, where, and when you will study. Find or create a work area where you can focus. And post your schedule somewhere visible so that those you live with know when you are studying and when you will make time for them.

5. You reduce distractions.

Don't answer texts, calls, or e-mails while studying.

6. You learn before you memorize.

Be fluent enough to explain all key rules simply and clearly to someone who has no legal background.

7. You avoid negative people.

Recognize the "negative voices" and avoid them.

8. You take practice tests in all of three subjects, working to continuously improve.

Every day, take practice tests under timed conditions. Study the explanatory answers to determine how to improve. Look up rules you don't know and write them out on flashcards and/or in an outline you use to help you study.

9. You prep for exam day.

Read all of the exam rules and instructions. Take care of everything else so that all you have to do is pass.

10. You have planned something fun after the exam.

Make sure that those who sacrificed with you have something to look forward to after the exam.

CHAPTER 2

DEVELOP YOUR PLAN TO PASS THE FYLSX

CHAPTER SUMMARY: This Chapter will introduce you to success planning strategies and guide you in drafting your initial FYLSX Success Plan.

Any big event requires plans. Would you host a wedding without planning? The FYLSX and a few years from now the Bar Exam are events that require advanced planning.

This chapter helps you draft your FYLSX plan. Like a business plan, your success plan should consider the **time, funding, and training** required to pass the FYLSX exam.

START BY LEARNING ABOUT YOUR FYLSX

Read everything from the Examiners and stay current. As of the time of the writing of this edition, the most up-to-date information is at https://www.calbar.ca.gov/Admissions/Examinations/First-Year-Law-Students-Examination. Bookmark this page and study every word. Return to the website frequently as you prefer for the exam.

Beware of old material: The Baby Bar changed significantly in 2024. It used to test with essays and MCQs and now only tests with MCQs.

In addition to learning what is tested:

- Complete the application, pay fees, and get a clear understanding of all testing rules and logistics by studying https://www.calbar.ca.gov/Admissions/Examinations/First-Year-Law-Students-Examination
- Review all the three tested subjects so that you thoroughly understand the law. And, take many practice multiple choice tests. Use Adaptibar for

multiple choice practice, and West's *Step-by-Step Guides* to Torts, Contracts, and Criminal Law to learn the law.

In addition to learning the law, you must train skills. The most important key to FYLSX success is critical reading. Detailed reading is perhaps the most important skill of both law students and practicing lawyers.

As you study, get into habits of using online annotation software and reading proactively with techniques such as:

1. Highlighting the words "***and***" and "***or***"
2. Underlining key terms
3. Writing your own thoughts as notes in the margins. (Do this with a stylus when reading online.)
4. Read aloud.
5. Look up words you do not know.
6. Reread paragraphs you don't understand.

"Before everything else, getting ready is the secret of success."

—HENRY FORD—

In addition to learning the law and training skills, take care of all other planning and logistics matters, such as those below, well before the exam.

Accommodations for Disabilities

Being granted accommodations for a disability in law school does not mean you will receive accommodations on the FYLSX or bar exam. If you have a disability and believe you would benefit from having accommodations on the exam, research what is required and how to make such a request, https://www.calbar.ca.gov/Admissions/Examinations/Requesting-Testing-Accommodations.

Mental Health or Substance Use

Get help if you need help. You are not alone. Consult your local lawyer assistance program (LAP) and find useful information in this free online pamphlet, *Substance Abuse & Mental Health Toolkit, for Law School Students and Those Who Care About Them*, available on the American Bar Association website.

Reading Challenges

If you need to improve reading skills or English language skills, seek help from a reliable resource at your law school.

Be Consistent

It's not the time to experiment with a new diet or to quit smoking or drinking coffee. Do those things if you want to *after* your FYLSX! But this is not a time to go cold turkey, especially on something on which you depend.

Don't Fall into the Useless Trap of Blaming Your Professors for Not Teaching Everything You Need to Know

They are teaching you how to learn what you need to know. You can easily pick up now what you haven't yet learned. This is your opportunity.

Start Exercising

You will need this stress release. If you have a routine, keep at it. If you don't, even a daily walk or any daily movement if you are unable to walk will help a lot.

Take Vacation Time to Prep for the Exam

Especially if you are working full time, consider part-time, flextime, or remote work opportunities. Look into vacation time, unpaid leave, and any other ways to free up as much time as possible to study during the month (and especially the week) before your FYLSX.

Draft Your Success Plan

Start filling in the information below.

FYLSX Success Target Date:

I am sitting for ***and will pass*** the FYLSX on

____

Signed— *[date]*

FYLSX Info:

This website is bookmarked on my laptop

https://www.calbar.ca.gov/Admissions/Examinations/First-Year-Law-Students-Examination

____

FYLSX deadlines:

The deadline for timely filing of my application to sit for the FYLSX and the date exam fees are due:

____

____

____

FYLSX Registration:

I have completed my exam registration requirements. ☐ Yes ☐ Not yet

About the FYLSX

Coverage: My exam tests the following subjects in MCQ format:

1. ____
2. ____
3. ____

My FYLSX Study Resources:

I am using the following materials to study:

____ Adaptibar

____ West *Step-by-Step Guides*

____ Other

My Dedicated FYLSX Time:

I have dedicated _____ hours per week to FYLSX exam study beginning _________, 20_____.

For working students: I have requested time off to focus on my FYLSX studies. ☐ Yes ☐ No

I still must find a way to put off or minimize the time I will spend on the following. (List commitments you are still figuring out how to defer, manage, delegate to others, or eliminate.)

____

____

____

Managing Distractions that take me away from FYLSX study:

I have identified the following as potentially taking time away from my studies, (for example, friends and family members who text me all the time):

____

____

____

My biggest distractions tend to be:

____

____

____

____

____

____

Written FYLSX Study Schedule:

I have a written study schedule ☐ Yes ☐ No

The following are places I can study effectively, without interruption (e.g., office, home, law library):

____

____

____

People in my inner circle know my study schedule so they know when I cannot be interrupted. ☐ Yes ☐ Not yet

My study schedule includes hours for specific tasks, such as:

- Actively reading and studying *Step-by-Step Guides* (or other outlines) ______
- Creating my own summary outlines (personalized "cheat sheets") ______
- Memorizing the law ______
- Completing MCQs under timed conditions and studying explanatory answers ______

Confidence and Motivation:

At this point, my greatest strengths going into exam preparation are:

1. ______________________________
2. ______________________________
3. ______________________________

At this point, my biggest challenges going into exam preparation are:

1. ______________________________
2. ______________________________
3. ______________________________

Other FYLSX Exam Planning Issues:

Health issues:

I have taken steps to deal with any health issues that might interfere with my ability to do my best on the exam. ☐ Yes ☐ No

I received accommodations in law school and expect to receive the same or similar accommodations on the exam and have thus completed all the necessary paperwork to apply for such accommodations. ☐ Yes ☐ No

I have had my vision and hearing checked in the past year. ☐ Yes ☐ No

Dependent care:

I have taken steps to arrange for any needed care for children, older or ill relatives, pets, etc. ☐ Yes ☐ No

HARD WORK IS NOT GLAMOROUS, BUT IT IS THE MOST IMPORTANT PART OF SUCCESS

Above all, the cornerstone of successful law study, successful law practice, and being a successful professional is and always will be *hard work*. There are no shortcuts.

Exam prep is a full-time job—even if you are training for the FYLSX on top of law school, work, and family obligations.

"The harder I work, the luckier I get."

—SAM GOLDWYN—

Think about it from another perspective. Let's say you were falsely accused of a crime and needed legal counsel. Would you want a lawyer willing to stay up all night to give you the best defense, or would you want someone looking for shortcuts?

Law school and the FYLSX, although they require a memorized bank of knowledge, are **not** about regurgitating facts.

They are about *reasoning*. They are about seeing how rules and principles *apply* to new facts, and *why* a particular outcome should result in each new situation.

You can and must learn and memorize a lot, but you also must take the time and effort necessary to develop your ability to skillfully apply law to facts and reason to logical conclusions.

Whatever your unique motivation, identifying your purpose for pursuing a law degree will help you get through the FYLSX exam.

Hard work is easier when you hold onto your dreams. It's a bit like tennis; your eyes must focus first on where the ball is coming from and then on where you want it to go with your stroke and follow-through. Here, too, you need to first look briefly back to when you began your studies and why you pursued a legal education, so you can then look confidently toward where you are heading.

FYLSX can feel like moving through an endless tunnel. Seeing the light will help you keep moving, taking the right steps, and doing the necessary follow-through to realize your full potential.

Weekly Time Tracking

Enter the time you spend each week on the following activities/tasks.

Remember, there are only 168 hours in a week!

Hours	Task
___	Work (include remote work).
___	Non-work-related communication (include texting, audio or video calls, and in-person visits with family/friends).
___	Family/friends commitments, including dinners, parties, celebrations, and helping relatives with errands or tasks for which they depend on you. Only log these once, so if you include these in another category below, leave this one blank.
___	Commute.
___	Exercise.
___	Religious observances, including prayer, services, holidays, weddings, bar mitzvahs, christenings, and the like. Be sure to log time for home observance.
___	Community, neighborhood, or other volunteer work.
___	Childcare, care of elderly or other relatives, pet care (including walking the dog).
___	Sleep.
___	Meal preparation (include shopping and cooking).
___	Eating meals (be sure to log the time to actually eat and social time around meals).
___	Self-care (showering, hair care, dressing) for you and dependents.
___	Health care (your own, and what you do for young children or others who depend on you).
___	Personal finance and record keeping (paying the bills, sorting mail, etc.).

___ Personal recreation and relaxation (TV, movies, social media, and whatever you do to unwind).

___ Other:

___ Subtotal:

___ *Study:*

___ Total:

Question (and be honest!): Does your list total more than 168 hours? How much time is allocated for study? Are you actually studying as much as you think you are? Study is intentionally listed last because people tend to inflate the time spent studying, and it is important to see how much time you really have left for study after everything else on your list.

Time Tips for Law Students Who Are Parents

Some students with families say they feel guilty that law school is taking them away from their kids. If this is you, know that your studying is positive role modeling. You are teaching discipline and the value of hard work through your actions.

Studies show that role modeling is more effective than preaching, so don't be surprised if your children do better in school when you are also studying.

Here are some other tips:

- If you have dependent children or aging parents who must be able to reach you in an emergency, give them special ringtone. You'll know if it's something you need to get to right away or if it can wait until you decide to take the study break you have earned by completing whatever tasks were on your schedule.
- Keep personal "office hours" (or "study hours") so your family knows when you are studying and not to be interrupted, and when you are available.
- Include your children, significant other, or parents in your studying when you can productively do so. Ask them to test you with flash cards. (Be prepared, your kids may memorize the rules before you do!)

- Play audio versions of books or lectures while you are driving, cooking, cleaning, or playing with your kids.
- Use flash cards app on your smartphone to test yourself if you are at the park or waiting in line at the market.
- If you have young children, read or sing your outlines aloud. Infants and toddlers mostly just want to hear your voice and be close to you. Whether you are reading *Goodnight Moon* or *The Step-by-Step Guide to Contracts* may not matter!
- Plan a fun after-exam trip or activity and let your kids (if age appropriate) decide what that will be.

Find a Good Study Spot

If your home is not conducive to studying, find a place suitable to concentrate, perhaps a local public library, bookstore, or café. Find your best "study spots" before intensive FYLSX review begins. Tip: you may need to stay somewhere other than home for the last week before the exam for total focus.

Do Not Buy Every Supplemental Resource You See

Too much information will distract you and waste your time. Worse still, some of that material may not be from reliable sources. Studying incorrect law is not only a waste (a neutral), but it will undo progress you have made (a severe negative—a time thief and an underminer.) If you get caught up in contradictory sources, you may find yourself more confused than ever and having to start over.

CHAPTER TAKEAWAYS: TOP TEN TIPS

1. "Believe you can PASS!"

Set your goal. Stick with it even if you are tempted to slip into thinking, "Well, I'll give it a shot, but I doubt I can pull it off with all the work and family commitments I am juggling." No!

2. Secure "buy-in" from others.

Help those in your support network to understand what your studying will entail. And, plan something fun to celebrate when the exam is done.

3. Start early.

You cannot cram for the FYLSX. Slow and steady wins the race.

4. Carve out several productive hours each day.

Determine when you study most productively and dedicate those hours to FYLSX prep exclusively. Post your study schedule so that anyone who wants your time knows when you may not be interrupted. Unless it's a true emergency, keep study time for studying.

5. Stay organized, disciplined, and committed to success.

Get systems in place to handle whatever must be done while you are studying. Put off everything that can wait until after the FYLSX.

6. Don't skimp on sleep, exercise, or motivating study breaks.

The exam is a physical and mental challenge. Be ready to perform at your best.

7. Protect your time. Protect your work space.

Study hours are precious. Do you hand over the keys to your home without very good reason to do so? Don't hand away your key to success: time!

If you have an office, desk, or other work space that is all yours, keep it that way. Do not share your computer with anyone. Don't open any attachments unless you are certain of their origin; keep spyware and antivirus protections up to date. The last thing you need is a virus in the weeks before the exam.

If you study in a coffee shop or library, don't leave your laptop unattended. We regularly hear stories about students losing or having laptops stolen just before the exam. Control what is in your control.

8. Reduce distractions.

Don't get sucked into anything unless it helps you study or recharges your batteries.

9. Set realistic expectations.

Do not rush yourself through study guides or practice tests. It is better to really learn what you're spending time on than to hastily skim the material and not really absorb it. When you are too tired to focus, switch tasks or take a nap.

10. Use every minute effectively.

Study when you study. Don't fall into the trap of feeling guilty that you are not studying when you are with family, and feeling guilty that you are not with family when you are studying. All that gets you is a lot of guilt and not a lot of effective studying. Be in the moment. Use commute time and exercise time to listen to lectures or recordings of your own voice reading rule statements.

CHAPTER 3

USE QUALITY RESOURCES

CHAPTER SUMMARY: This Chapter highlights the types and quality of resources needed to pass the FYLSX.

This book is about achieving. It is about success. It is not about pipe dreams. Nowhere am I saying, "Just be confident, and you will pass."

Some goals are easier to achieve with the help of experts. FYLSX passage is one of those. You must learn, memorize, and be able to clearly articulate many rules and concepts. You must master numerous skills, including critical reading, factual and legal analysis, and time management. It helps to use materials created by experts who know what they are talking about. Conversely, it is an act of sabotage to solicit (and often pay dearly for) misinformation. Going it alone or with an unreliable tutor may means the difference between succeeding or not.

Beware. If anyone promises you a foolproof, quick, or easy system to pass the FYLSX, walk away. Quality instructors, like personal trainers, do *not* make it easy. They keep you on track. Reliable experts will tell you there are no shortcuts. Studying just is hard work.

PERSONALIZE YOUR REVIEW MATERIALS

One of the best ways to be learn and retain what you need for the exam is to personalize the content. What do I mean?

- Take good notes that make sense to you.
- Write in your books or use electronic note-taking systems for online materials.
- Draw diagrams and pictures, if helpful. (Many find visuals useful in real property.)
- Add hypotheticals or examples that illustrate a rule in a way that makes sense to you.

- Translate formal rule statements into plain English short phrases to help you learn them.
- Make your own flash cards or personalize flash cards that you buy. Write the legal term on the front. On the back, write both a succinct and proper phrasing of the rule and a plain-English simple phrasing of the rule *that make sense to you.*

Self-Assessment: Personalized Flash Cards

If the front of the flashcard says, "*The law that governs contract disputes,*" note what you would write on the back in the space below.

Hopefully you wrote something such as: "*Contract disputes may be governed by different bodies of law depending on the nature of the dispute. Where the dispute regards movable goods, the governing law is typically the Uniform Commercial Code or UCC, whereas disputes about land or services are typically governed by the common law.*"

Now, take a moment to think about how this makes sense to you, in your own words.

You might think: UCC—transactions in goods—moveable things like refrigerators or "widgets." Common law—basically land (Blackacre) or services (doing something). UCC may be influential even when not controlling. Remember tricky fact patterns, such as "growing crops" are considered land, but when harvested or severed from the land, they are considered goods. Also, for mixed UCC and common law contracts, remember the practice question with Builder who supplied wood (goods) and with that wood built a fence (services). If mixed, can I divide into two contracts? If not, which predominates, goods or services?

Personalizing your flash cards (or writing notes such as these in the margins of your outlines) will help you master simple and complex points alike and prepare you to apply your learning to practice tests. Be sure to have flash cards or personalized notes on every heavily tested concept, and make cards every time you get a practice question wrong because you did not know or understand a rule. Make sure your notes make sense to you. Let's try another example.

What is *consideration*?
Formal definition:

Define in your own words so you understand:

MAKE SURE YOU UNDERSTAND WHAT YOU HEAR AND READ

This is a basic premise. When we don't know what certain terms mean, we can't readily understand explanations of concepts that use those terms. But how often do we stop and look them up? Too often we just move on and hope we will "get it" from context clues. That *may* work for leisure reading, but it does not work for law.

From now on, plan to learn rules and definitions just as you would learn vocabulary to become fluent in a foreign language. When you are not certain of the meaning of a legal term, stop and look it up. Remember that some terms seem familiar but have different meanings when used in the legal context. (The word *consideration* is a great example.)

Deep understanding will help you to memorize and to spot the significance of rules in MCQ fact patterns.

Quick Rule Memorization Test

Explain felony murder to a very smart 16-year-old—or any intelligent non-lawyer.

CHAPTER 4

IT TAKES A VILLAGE OF POSITIVE PEOPLE

CHAPTER SUMMARY: This Chapter helps determine who understands you and who will be supportive, and helps provide strategies to deal with people who are not supportive.

"Do what you feel in your heart to be right, for you'll be criticized anyway. You'll be damned if you do and damned if you don't."

—ELEANOR ROOSEVELT—

We talked in previous chapters about believing in yourself and your ability to pass, and investing in yourself so you have the resources to succeed. This chapter discusses the importance of having a supportive network.

So, who are the people in your world? Who makes up your "team," your support system, your inner circle? The first part of this analysis involves some triage. Start by sorting people into three categories:

- people who are supportive and "get it" right away;
- people who will support you but need help learning how to be supportive; and
- people who will not be helpful or may be downright destructive. (I call these, "saboteurs.")

Learn to rely primarily during your intensive study times on those who are already supportive. It is easier to surround yourself with people who "get it."

There may be people you cannot enlist for support now but who will come around eventually. They may even end up being huge supporters later in your life and career. But right now, they don't get it, and they will not help you pass the FYLSX.

Know that you are not alone if friends or family are not supportive. Your best strategy may be to express understanding so as to not feel angry or bitter yourself and let go of any expectation of support from such persons now. Approach them if you wish to later, after the exam. In the meantime, find at least one person who *is* supportive and reach out to that person now, so you have someone in your corner.

Some people mean well and want to help but don't know how. It can be beneficial to enlist the support of your immediate circle of family and friends, but sometimes you need to guide them. Unless they are lawyers, they will likely have a hard time understanding the intensity of your studies. Even other professionals, such as doctors and accountants, often don't get it.

Still another level of challenge arises if you live with someone who doesn't get it. Let's say it's your parent or partner. If you are not able to help that person understand what you need, your best strategy may be to study at a library, an empty room in your law school, or any place conducive to focus that is outside your home.

To help people understand your situation, I drafted the following letter. Feel free to use it if it helps.

FAMILY/FRIENDS LETTER

Dear Friend, Family, or Significant Other:

Someone close to you will be taking the FYLSX exam in a few months. Obviously, each person and each family facing this experience differs, but there are parallels. Here are just some of the challenges your person faces and what has worked for others like you who want to be supportive. Think of this as both a success and survival note—you want your person to pass the exam, and you want to survive this long haul!

Start with the "long haul." This a huge challenge. It is sort of like a "Mount Everest climb." One does not reach the summit without proper gear and training. Your person cannot give the exam short shrift. It requires total commitment, 100 percent focus, and a great deal of time.

- Expect your person to be "gone" prior to the exam. Note: Your person may be present physically, but in another mental space altogether.
- Your person will think about exam fact patterns while eating, showering, and sleeping—dreaming (or having nightmares).
- The person you knew as perhaps a slightly crazed law student will be taken over totally by a disease that I call "examitis." The good news is it's temporary!
- Your person is in a fierce and exhausting competition. Some people in that competition are doing nothing but study.

After the exam, your person will return mentally as well as physically; it will be a time to reconnect. In the meantime:

- Say "No" in advance to all social commitments for your person.
- Be flexible and willing as much as possible to play every day by ear. If at the last minute your person has put in a productive enough study day that he or she is able to join in a social event, be welcoming. But understand that even if your person has finished studying for the day, he or she may need to sleep, exercise, or just unwind.
- Delay important decisions, significant changes, major purchases, and arguments until after the exam. (This is not the time to buy a new house, refinance a home, or remodel.) Anything that can wait, let it wait.
- Make life during exam prep as easy as possible. Some exam takers who are parents of young children ship their kids off to grandparents for a vacation to make more study time. Many use paper plates for every meal. You get the idea.
- Help your person get on and stay on a study schedule. If you have a family, it will often be helpful for your person to be available on a

consistent and predictable basis, even for thirty minutes. Encourage your person to set and keep "family hours." It will help to know that "Mom or Dad is studying but will be there for you at least a few minutes at 7:00 p.m. every night [or for breakfast every morning]."

- Participate, if there is any interactive studying that would help. For example, be willing to test your person with flash cards or listen to lectures in the car or while cooking. Be open to listening if your person needs to vent.
- Accommodate your person's needs as fully as possible during the week of their exam. If he or she needs to be alone, respect that. If he or she needs you there, try to be there.
- Note: If your person is not clearly expressing what will make him or her the most well prepared, well rested, and confident going in to the exam, ask. Remind your person that you are not mind readers.
- Last but not least, do not take personally any moodiness and tension. Stress comes with the exam. This too shall pass.

Sincerely,

Bottom line: take the time to explain to the people you want to support you the situation that you are in as you study for the Baby Bar. Let them know in advance exactly what you are facing and precisely what sort of support you need.

"Success is that peace of mind that comes from knowing you've done everything in your power to become the very best you're capable of becoming."

—JOHN WOODEN—

NEGATIVE PEOPLE—FRIENDS OR STRANGERS

When faced with a negative person during exam preparation, the best advice is to get away.

There will be people who are just dying to tell you about everyone they know—from their neighbor's son to famous people—who failed a bar exam. They might then say, "And, that was the *real* bar; you're only taking the *baby* bar. How hard could that be?!" Walk away. Don't listen. As I've said, the Baby Bar is not a baby anything. It is a super hard exam, and unless someone has taken it, their opinion should not matter. (And, ever those who have taken it are not you. You are running your own race.)

Sometimes it can be even more stressful when people make seemingly positive comments, such as, "Oh, I know you'll pass." To many applicants, that just piles on more stress by adding expectations you must live up to. How should you respond? One of my students shared that she would simply reply, "I'm doing my best," and either walk away or change the subject.

KEEP DOUBTERS AT A DISTANCE: BUILD A PROTECTIVE WALL AROUND YOUR SELF-CONFIDENCE

How should you deal with people you intuitively know are seeking to undermine your self-confidence or steal your study time? Take steps to keep strong—in mind, body, and spirit. Passing the exam is in some ways like climbing a mountain. Because it's such a challenge, there may be days when you ask yourself, "Can I do it?" Remind yourself that if you were not the kind of person who thrived when challenged, you would not have started law school.

Relatives and Others Making Destructive Comments

If you need a boost, or a pep talk, ask a trusted professor, mentor, or classmate.

If people in your family or community do not support you, *do not* look to them for support now. Do not "buy in" to their negativity. You have every right to be proud of earning a law degree and seeking to obtain a law license.

If you have negative folks in your life, don't try to change their minds right now. First pass the exam, with the help of supportive people, and *then* try to bring them around.

Self-Assessment: Supporters and Saboteurs

Complete this exercise, thinking about and noting who is and is not supportive in the spaces below. Don't show anyone. Delete these lists after you write them. But clarifying for yourself who will help and who won't, can greatly increase your productivity.

Part A: List your supportive troops (Write the names of and contact info for people you know "get it," whom you can call or reach out to when you need a boost.):

1.
2.
3.
4.
5.

Part B: List people who are supportive, but don't yet "get it":

1.
2.
3.
4.
5.

Part C: List potential saboteurs, people you find unsupportive:

1.
2.
3.
4.
5.

Part D: List actual saboteurs, people to avoid altogether:

1. ____
2. ____

3. ______________________________
4. ______________________________
5. ______________________________

CHAPTER 5

MAXIMIZE PRODUCTIVITY

CHAPTER SUMMARY: This Chapter provides strategies to help take control of your time and reduce distractions.

SAMPLE EARLY START STUDY SCHEDULE FOR WORKING STUDENTS OR THOSE WITH LIMITED TIME

The following are suggestions on what to complete each week for several months leading up to the exam:

- Fifty multiple choice questions—reviewing explanatory answers, noting what you missed and why. Make flash cards for and/or update your outline with difficult-to-remember rules. When you begin studying, you can do this practice one subject at a time; as the exam approaches, mix up the topics.
- Study *Step-by-Step Guides to contracts, torts, and criminal law*, one every two weeks.

One month before the exam

- One hour before work: Complete seventeen multiple choice questions in thirty minutes. Review the explanatory answers for thirty minutes, writing flash cards for rules you missed.
- One hour at lunch: Complete another seventeen multiple choice questions in thirty minutes. Review the explanatory answers for thirty minutes.
- One hour immediately after work: Complete another set of MCQs. (Especially if home is distracting, it can be helpful to stay at or near work, or go to a coffee shop if you work remotely, and get in an extra couple of hours before you head home.)

- Use commute time (if any) to listen to lectures or review and memorize rules.
- Read *Step-by-Step Guides,* take notes, and make flashcards.

While some people can work a full day, eat dinner, and then study productively for four to five hours straight, many working students find it easier to spread tasks throughout the day, putting in at least some time before, during, and after work as described above. Try both approaches and see which one is more effective for you.

On weekends or non-work days, suggestions for tasks include:

- Study full days, from 9:00 a.m. to 6:00 p.m., with at least one hour for lunch. Combine lectures and looking up rules with additional practice MCQ exams.
- Take off evenings for rest and relaxation so you don't burn out and so you will have just as much energy the next day.

DAILY SCHEDULES VERSUS WEEKLY SCHEDULES

Most people prefer daily schedules. For those studying full time, daily schedules leave no time to waste deciding what to do. You get up, do your work at the same time each day, and fall in to a productive routine. Even if you are working, write a daily schedule for yourself if your schedule is consistent each day. If you have to adapt it, write down any changes so that they also become tasks that must be completed.

For working students whose commitments vary from day to day, a weekly schedule may be most effective. Let's say you plan to complete seventeen MCQs in a half hour each morning during breakfast and thirty-three questions in an hour on weekend days, plus allow time to review following each practice session. If you can't always commit to this because some days you have more work than others, consider a weekly schedule with at least 200 MCQs per week plus review time. (Note: These numbers may be *minimums*! You can always do more. But it is more effective to do a consistent number on a regular basis than a marathon session once a week.)

One former student whose erratic work schedule interfered with accomplishing daily tasks felt like a failure, though he had multiple engineering degrees and decades of experience in demanding jobs. He decided to switch to a weekly schedule. He completed more on lighter work days and less on busier ones, and got everything on his study list done by week's end. This allowed him to once again think of himself as the success he was, and still is.

Simply changing *when* you do things may make you think of yourself in a different light.

THE INGREDIENTS OF A SUCCESSFUL SCHEDULE

What goes into an effective study schedule? Ideally, you should build in law study, skills training, self-care including exercise, sleep, and good nutrition, and a little bit of relaxation and fun to "replenish the well."

Rough Draft Schedule

Drawing upon what you now know about yourself and how and when you learn best, try to sketch out an effective schedule.

6 a.m.
7 a.m.
8 a.m.
9 a.m.

10 a.m.
11 a.m.
Noon
1 p.m.
2 p.m.
3 p.m.
4 p.m.
5 p.m.
6 p.m.
7 p.m.

8 p.m.	
9 p.m.	
10 p.m.	
11 p.m.	

VARIETY

Studying in different ways can enhance learning. Shaking things up can also prevent burnout and get you through some long, tough days.

Change locations once or twice a week. As a reward for studying well in your regular study spot, bring your device outdoors, perhaps somewhere with a great view, or to a favorite coffee shop.

Vary your study techniques. Variety alone may help you stay on course; adding some fun may help even more. For example:

- Talk through concepts or rules you don't understand with a friend, study buddy, or mentor (perhaps over coffee). If it is someone who will stay focused and not distract you, the person doesn't have to have a legal background. (As noted previously, if you can explain something clearly to a layperson, you are ready to use that concept in an essay on the exam.)
- Set some of your mnemonics, checklists, or summary outlines to music. Memorize rules by singing them to the melody of a popular tune.

- Make charts and diagrams.
- Include some funny images (perhaps a cartoon that makes you laugh) in your study materials.
- Make a recording of yourself reading key rules out loud. Hearing your own voice confidently stating rules will have an empowering effect, even if you were reading the rules when you made the recording.

Making Study More Enjoyable

In the space below, list three things you can do to switch up your studying to make it more fun for you. Use the suggestions above or your own ideas.

1. ______________________________

2. ______________________________

3. ______________________________

Don't expect each day to be miraculous. Expect it to be hard work. A lot of your preparation may seem like drudgery, but every bit of effort is worth the spectacular payoff down the road. Expect to be tired. Keep pushing forward anyway.

Be determined. Keep your goal, your "endgame," in mind. You are in training. It's not supposed to be easy. Learn as you go, one day at a time. Trust that if you put in what it takes, you will get where you need to go.

Use every good moment you have to study, sleep, or otherwise prepare. Don't waste time fooling yourself. If you are not effectively using your time, get on the ball. Don't spin your wheels. When you hit a wall (and you will!), change gears or stop and take a break.

Don't quit or get discouraged at the first signs of losing focus. You need to build your stamina. Push yourself. It's not easy. But when you find yourself reading the same thing over and over, looking out the window and not "hearing" yourself, take a break. Maybe take a nap. Sometimes after even a short sleep, you can get back in gear and be more productive. Above all, remain patient. Keep moving forward.

Work hard. Work steadily. Work smart. Work when others are goofing off. And do not waste one moment feeling sorry for yourself that you *have to* work while others play. You *get to* work. And you will get to reap the future rewards of that hard work.

Pace yourself and don't burn out. Do what it takes to keep moving forward, slowly but steadily, on this road to success.

What should you do when you're blocked by anxiety? That depends on when the nerves hit. Let's consider different strategies for different times you find yourself getting nervous.

ANXIETY WHILE TAKING PRACTICE ESSAY TESTS

If paralyzing anxiety prevents forward movement while you are taking a practice test, the immediate mission is to get the intellectual flow going again—to take the edge off. Try simply reading aloud. That may break the temporary paralysis. Try pouring yourself a cup of tea. Or try standing up and sitting back down every so often.

ANXIETY-REDUCING TOOLS TO USE ANY TIME NERVES HIT

Some techniques work particularly well during an exam. Other strategies are helpful any time you feel anxious.

These simple steps will help when nerves hit:

- Breathe. Slow, steady, deep breaths will often release the nerves and "paralysis" that comes from them. We tend to tense up when we are nervous, and often forget to breathe properly. You will read more clearly and think more clearly when the oxygen is flowing freely.
- Visualize yourself on the exam, answering multiple choice questions confidently, feeling in control.
- Talk to yourself positively. Positive thinking is critical! Tell yourself every day that you *can* do this. Say it aloud several times each day. Banish from your mind any past test-taking experiences that were not positive. Replace them with empowering images of you conquering challenges.

It is important to develop some effective calming habits that you can employ if you find yourself panicking *on the actual exam.*

Breathing and self-talk techniques help—along with *the most effective tool to combat nerves: adequate preparation.* The better your training, the more prepared you are, the less your nerves will hinder you. If you do feel nervous, which is normal no matter how hard you have studied, you will be much more able to turn the anxiety into adrenaline so it serves, rather than defeats, you. (Remember my three Ps: turn *panic* into *power* not *paralysis!*)

Selecting Study Spots

Worksheet

1. Are you studying in a coffee shop? Some find this great but others get distracted people watching. How is it working for you?

2. Are you studying in your home? Is it quiet? Do you have a dedicated study space? (If you are doing more housework or distracted by things in your home, try studying somewhere else for a bit.)

3. Is the place you are studying helping you focus? Why or why not?

HOW TO MEMORIZE? BREAK OUT THE FLASHCARDS, WRITE IT FIFTY TIMES, DO WHATEVER WORKS FOR YOU!

Especially if you find you are missing MCQs that are testing the same or similar areas of law, it may mean that you just don't understand those rules. Read and reread rule statements aloud. Create hypotheticals or examples that illustrate the rule in context. Engage fully in the memorization process. In the smartphone age, our memories take the back seat. We don't need them much, if at all. But by exam time, your mind needs to act as a sort of "Siri" or "Alexa" for legal rules. You will need at your command a clear understanding of all testable rules in all three subjects.

PREVENTING BURNOUT: ADD INCENTIVES AND LEVITY

Studying for high stakes exams is a test of endurance. You have to put in many high-gear days and pack into your brain more learning than you ever thought you could absorb, and you have to do this day in and day out. This section provides suggestions to help stay on course and not burn out.

REWARD YOURSELF

Give yourself a small but consistent reward *each day* for doing your best, and a slightly bigger one each week for sticking to your schedule.

Rewarding Yourself for Your Hard Work

Worksheet

List how you might reward yourself for a job well done. Some suggestions: Watch mindless TV; have a great meal with a glass of wine; go out for a movie and popcorn; take a walk outdoors (try repeating a motivational saying as you walk); go someplace where you can see the ocean, a beautiful mountain, or some other scenery that takes you out of your day-to-day; laugh with a supportive friend; or eat some delicious chocolate. (I know that chocolate won't add brain cells, but it may well lift your mood and put a smile on your face.)

What is a reward for you?

____

____

____

We talked earlier about anxiety and how to combat nerves. What about fatigue and burnout? First, let's address the differences between these. It is one of degree. If you are just tired, sleeping more may help. For anxiety, try the tips discussed earlier. (Note that you are apt to be more nervous and less able to conquer anxiety when you are tired.) If you are suffering from burnout, recharging your batteries may be a bit more difficult.

What can you do about burnout? First, admit it. Face it so you can correct it. Allowing yourself to be so "done" that you are blocked from putting in further effort will not result in success.

Next, assess whether it's a major burnout and you need help from a trained professional. Or, do you just need a day or possibly a few days away? If you know that you are too fried to focus, take time off. Get some fresh air. Change the scenery. Clear your mind.

For minor burnout, try giving yourself consistent small rewards and breaks that you know you can look forward to after every productive study day. It can also be helpful to break up the day. Put in a focused study block in the morning; then take a good, long lunch. Eat something healthy, hydrate, get some exercise, or take a nap if you need it.

Take a similar break following afternoon and evening study sessions. Spend time with someone supportive, if you have someone in your life who is helpful. If not, spend any downtime with a good book or movie! (Do not spend time with anyone who saps your energy or keeps you from meeting your goal.)

MOTIVATE WITH MUSIC

Every time you feel overwhelmed, overloaded, tired, fearful, or discouraged, play music or hum a song to yourself that makes your spirit sing.

WHAT IS ON YOUR EXAM PLAYLIST?

What is on your exam playlist? ____________________

If you don't have an exam playlist, make one!

FINALIZING YOUR SCHEDULE

Update the draft schedule you wrote earlier. Be sure your schedule includes regular disciplined study *and* regular breaks to recharge your batteries. Post this final schedule somewhere you and anyone you live with will see it every day.

6 a.m.
7 a.m.
8 a.m.
9 a.m.
10 a.m.
11 a.m.
Noon
1 p.m.
2 p.m.
3 p.m.
4 p.m.

5 p.m.
6 p.m.
7 p.m.
8 p.m.
9 p.m.
10 p.m.

CHAPTER 6

PRACTICE TESTS: THE HEAVY LIFTING

CHAPTER SUMMARY: This Chapter provides strategies for success multiple choice questions. Note: As of June 2024, FYLSE no longer contains essay questions and is comprised only of 100 multiple choice questions (MCQs). Because you will still have essay exams in law school, the Chapter also includes some essay success strategies. Mastering these will in turn improve your MCQ skills; you will gain greater understanding and be able to pull back the curtain of "mysteries" behind each testing format. Practicing with essays also helps you learn the law well.

"I WISH I HAD STARTED EARLIER!"

Biggest tip ever: Don't wait until the last minute. You cannot cram for this exam. I would be quite wealthy if I had a dollar for every student who said, "I wish I had started sooner." Don't think you can cram for the FYLSX. Slow and steady wins this race. Get to be an MCQ expert by putting in many hours of training. Start now!

THE MULTIPLE CHOICE QUESTIONS

These questions begin with a short fact pattern. The facts are followed by an interrogatory (question) and four answer choices. Applicants are to respond by choosing the best of the choices.

MCQ STRATEGY AND PREPARATION

To successfully answer MCQs:

- Cover the answer choices so you don't get suckered into selecting a seductive-looking answer before you even know the facts, and so that you do not become biased while reading the facts.

- Next, (with the answer choices covered), read the interrogatory or "call of the question," at or near at the end of the facts. This will help you know what area of law and hopefully the subtopic within that area you are in so that you can "call up" the relevant rules in your mind's search engine. (It is helpful if you can see not only is this a contracts question, for example, but it is testing formation.)
- Then read the fact pattern *and reread the interrogatory*. Remember to read critically, read with a stylus (or pencil if working on paper) in hand, touching and subvocalizing each word as you read. Underline words that trigger legal issues. Based on the law you have memorized, reason through the facts to draw a conclusion that you believe best answers the precise question asked.
- Only after completing these steps (including carefully re-reading the interrogatory) should you then take your hand off the answer choices and read through the first choice carefully, asking yourself:
    - "Is this choice plausible?"
    - "Is it responsive to the question?"
    - "Does it mirror the answer I reasoned to?"
    - "Is it even a correct statement in and of itself?"

  If the choice contains an incorrect rule statement, does not answer the question asked, or answers it incorrectly (applies the law incorrectly to these specific facts), immediately put a line through it and go on to the next choice.
- Ask yourself the same questions regarding each of the three remaining answer choices, crossing out any that are wrong or don't answer the question. Do this clearly so that you don't mistakenly think an answer choice is still on the table if you have ruled it out. (Some people find it helpful to play a sort of "find the wrong answers" game with themselves.

The more you rule out, the better. If you like puzzles, this might be a good strategy for you.)

- Now, what are you left with? If only one answer choice remains, select that one and quickly move on to the next question. (Always keep in mind that this is a test of speed as well as knowledge and accuracy, so keep moving.) If you have two answer choices that are both consistent with your conclusion but for different reasons, read each one again carefully and isolate what exactly differs between the two choices. Then see if one includes faulty reasoning, an internal inconsistency, an incorrect rule statement, or fails to answer the exact question posed. Re-read the interrogatory to be sure you understand the exact question. Re-read the facts as necessary. By process of elimination, choose the best of the remaining answers.
- Note that the best answer might not be perfect. Sometimes the best answer is supported by a minority rule rather than the prevailing majority rule. In such a situation, if the other choices are flat-out wrong, then the minority position will be the best answer. Select the answer that seems to reason to the best conclusion when applying appropriate law to resolve the issue asked in the particular question.
- When you study explanatory answers, you should strive to determine why you chose the answer you did, and, if you didn't choose the correct answer, why it was not the best choice and why the correct answer was best. (More on the self-assessment process below.)

PRACTICE BY COMPLETING A CONSISTENT NUMBER OF MCQs EVERY DAY, UNDER TIMED CONDITIONS

"How many should I take?" Students always ask this question—a difficult one to answer. The key is consistency. When I sit down with students to plan their schedules, I don't tell them how many to take each day. Rather, I ask them, "How much time do you have each day to commit to practice?" Once we have a time slot, we can figure out how many they should take each day.

Let's say you say, "I can devote a half hour every morning. I'll complete them while having coffee or breakfast." Then, you'll complete 17 questions in those 30 minutes daily, then find time later that day to review the explanatory answers and make flashcards for every rule you did not know or understand well.

Note: A guess is equivalent to a wrong answer in practice. If you guess right, you simply got lucky. Do not bank on luck; invest in knowledge, skill, and preparation.

STRATEGIC THINKING

You must answer 100 multiple choice questions. These questions require fast-paced reading and thinking. These questions test fine distinctions in points of law. You will need to choose the *best* answer for each question; therefore, *a single-most accurate* answer choice must necessarily be included for each question.

To make it possible that one answer is clearly the best, questions are often crafted such that the answer turns on a rule of law rather than a factual analysis. (Contrast this with law school essays which often focus more on facts from which differing inferences may be drawn. In other words, on an essay, taking the same facts, you could reason through them differently and end up with different conclusions. But there is no room to argue the facts when answering a MCQ; there is one and only one "best" answer.

Let's make this contrast clear with an example. If law school essay writing, you must explicitly state the inferences you make. Take a simple hypothetical criminal law scenario:

> *Defendant Dan is approached by Vicious Victor, who is wielding a knife. Uncertain as to whether Victor intends to kill Dan, Dan nonetheless responds by pulling out a gun; Dan shoots at Victor, aiming at Victor's toe. Victor dies as a result of the injury.*

Now, imagine an MCQ asks for Dan's best defense theory, with the following choices: (a) deadly weapon, (b) insanity, (c) self-defense, or (d) intoxication. Well, there are no facts to help Dan establish either an insanity or intoxication defense, so rule out choices "b" and "d." Next, although it isn't certain that Dan would prevail in asserting self-defense as a justification, it is likely the *best* of the choices. Why? The focus of the question is Dan's defenses, and Victor's use of a deadly weapon does not in and of itself provide a defense theory. In fact, it might help the prosecutor to convict Dan of a more serious offense, as discussed below. Note: This is tricky because Victor's use of a knife, a deadly weapon, is necessary to justify Dan having responded by defending himself with deadly force. But because the question asks what *Dan's best defense theory* would be, the best response appears to be "(c) self-defense."

The best answer would be less certain, however, if this same fact pattern were part of a law school essay question asking, "Of what crimes, if any, might Dan be convicted—and why?" The prosecutor would assert that Dan committed murder, and, unless Dan successfully argued a defense or mitigation theory, Dan would be convicted of either first- or second-degree murder. A murder is a homicide committed with malice aforethought. Dan killed Victor; therefore, Dan committed the homicide element of murder—that is, the killing of one human being by another. Dan's use of a deadly weapon allows for an *inference* that Dan possessed the intent to kill, which would prove malice and satisfy the mental state element of murder. (This means the judge or jury *could* find that Dan intended to kill Victor just because Dan used a deadly weapon in a deadly manner, without other evidence of Dan's actual intent. This does not have to be the conclusion, but it is permissible.)

Law students will correctly recognize that for a first-degree murder conviction, the prosecution would also have to establish that Dan's shooting was premeditated and deliberate. Both premeditation and deliberation would likely be more difficult to prove under these facts, as Dan's actions appear to have been unplanned. But before we even address these concerns, is it crystal clear that Dan had the required mental state? Not at all.

The prosecution *might* be able to show by virtue of using a deadly weapon that Dan possessed the intent to kill, but that is not the only reasonable inference one could draw. (And the judge or jury would not have to come to the same conclusion.) The defense could counter (or rebut) the inference that Dan intended to kill Victor, for example, by stressing that Dan aimed at Victor's toe.

What inference would be drawn from the fact that Dan shot at Victor's toe? Well, one who intends to kill typically aims for the head or a vital organ, rather than the smallest of extremities, right? So, Dan's having shot at Victor's toe might tend to prove that Dan did not intend to kill.

The prosecution might in turn contend that shooting at any part of a victim's body evidences an intent to kill or, at the very least an intent to seriously injure, a mental state that would suffice for second-degree murder.

The defense might go on to argue that Dan's actions were justified, that he was acting in self-defense. After all, Victor was the first to draw a weapon, his knife. But, in order to prevail in a complete self-defense justification, the defendant would have to prove that at the time of action, the defendant reasonably and in good faith feared being attacked with imminent deadly force. This could pose a problem for Dan. Why? Well, although it's true that Victor was wielding a deadly weapon himself, the facts specifically state that Dan was "uncertain" as to whether Victor was intending to kill him. (Maybe Victor wanted to show Dan his knife to prove how vicious he was, without intending to *use* the knife at all.) Unless Dan could establish that he himself believed, and that a reasonable person in his shoes would have believed, that he was about to be attacked by Victor with deadly force, it is doubtful Dan would prevail in claiming self-defense.

Therefore, a logical conclusion to the analysis might be that Dan would *likely* be convicted of second-degree murder because he shot Victor with what can be established as the intent to seriously injure. But it's *possible* to have logically concluded that despite aiming at Victor's toe, Dan still likely possessed the intent to kill, especially given his use of a deadly weapon.

From this short scenario and the fact that we were able to reason to more than one plausible conclusion, you can see how much more room there is for gray areas in essay questions than in MCQs. Learning the differences between the two and taking many practice tests will help you gain a command of effective test-taking strategies.

Remember, on MCQs your sole task is to find the *best* answer, but on essays you may reason to different conclusions depending on the inferences you logically draw from the facts, and whether the facts prove or disprove the existence of legal elements. All this to say, strategy-wise, your preparation for the FYLSE is different than your preparation for law school exams.

HOW TO SELF-ASSESS MCQs

First, be sure to keep track of which answers you felt fairly certain about and those on which you guessed. Be honest! Again, a guess on a practice exam is equivalent to a missed answer.

When you finish each practice set, study the answers. Don't just score yourself and add up the totals. The numbers (especially early on in your studying) aren't what count; the learning is what is critical. (It does not matter what the score was at halftime. *Focus on winning the game.*)

Proceed to work through every question you missed or guessed the answer. Read the explanatory answers, and most important, figure out *why* you missed the question. Note: You may miss a question for more than one reason.

Self-Assessment: MCQ Diagnostic

Check all boxes that apply:

- ☐ I read the question (the interrogatory) incorrectly.
- ☐ I missed a key word or words in the fact pattern.
- ☐ I read one or more answer choices incorrectly.
- ☐ I didn't understand what the question was asking, or I didn't see the issue.
- ☐ I didn't know the law that I needed to apply to the issue to reason to a conclusion.

- ☐ I memorized the rule, but I didn't understand the underlying principles the question was testing (so I narrowed it down to two possible choices, but I missed the best one).
- ☐ I knew the correct answer, but I entered it incorrectly.

Next, use this information *to improve*. (After explaining how to do this, I'll give you a chart to do on your own.) *Don't spend a minute being down on yourself or frustrated by the fact that you got the wrong answers.* That's a waste of time. So long as you know *why*, you are winning this game. (The word *game* does not suggest this is easy. But it can be helpful to view these as puzzles you are determined to solve.)

Practice tests are learning opportunities; your critical reading skills will become more refined and your reasoning more strategic with every set you do. (They are like weightlifting; train consistently, and you will get stronger.)

Be very pleased with yourself simply because you are *taking* daily practice tests. Do not obsess about scores. Just keep doing the work and self-assessing. Your goal is to develop strategies to strengthen different skill or knowledge gaps.

Reading Error?

If you read something incorrectly, ask yourself why. Did you read too fast? Did you drift off while reading? Did you assume some fact that was not in the fact pattern? Did you not understand the meaning of one or more words that turned out to affect the entire question? Which part of the question did you read incorrectly: the call, the facts, or the answer choices? (And, again, why did you miss that part? Were you rushing?) Once you know why you missed a question, you can then take steps to change the behavior. Reading incorrectly is one of the most common reasons for missed answers, and the easiest to fix.

Didn't Know or Understand a Rule?

If, after studying explanatory answers, you can see that you did not know or understand a rule, go look it up and either write it in your outline, on your paper, or electronic flash cards, or say it out loud several times, or both. (If you want to be sure you understand it, try explaining the concept to someone else.)

Expect to be learning some new rules from practice, even up to the day before the exam.

> USE EXPLANATORY ANSWERS TO CONTINUOUSLY UPDATE FLASHCARDS
>
> Even when you do understand a rule or concept, pay attention to explanatory answers that phrase rules in particularly clear or succinct language, or provide an instructive example. These are gifts. Get out your flash cards and rewrite your rule, replacing your old definition with the newer, clearer version.

Didn't Finish in Time?

If you didn't have time to carefully complete each question or didn't finish in the allotted time and guessed on several questions, ask yourself why. First, are you timing yourself? On the exam, you have approximately 1.8 minutes per question. Did you lose time by focusing too long on one question? Guess, and move on if you find you have spent more than 1.8 minutes on a question. Did you zone out while reading? Each set of questions is an opportunity to incrementally improve your accuracy and speed and your ability to focus for longer and more concentrated periods of time.

Self-Assessment: MCQ Chart to Track Wrong Answers (including guesses!)

Complete this assessment for every question you missed, checking the reason(s) you erred and writing an improvement plan, so that you do not repeat the same mistakes.

Question # ___

- ☐ I read the question (the interrogatory) incorrectly.
- ☐ I missed or misunderstood a key word or words in the fact pattern.
- ☐ I read one or more answer choices incorrectly.
- ☐ I did not understand what the question was asking or did not see what was at issue.
- ☐ I did not know the law that I needed to apply to the issue to reason to a conclusion. (If you missed a question because you didn't know the rule, write it now in the space below.)
- ☐ I memorized the rule, but didn't understand the underlying principles the question was testing (so I narrowed the answer down to two possible choices, but didn't choose the best one.)
- ☐ I knew the correct answer, but I entered it incorrectly.
- ☐ Other: ______________________________

To improve, I will:

____

____

____

Rule(s)/concept/area of law tested in this question that I need to learn/ memorize are:

____

____

____

Self-Assessment: MCQ Chart to Track Correct Answers

You can also benefit from reviewing questions you got right. Complete this assessment for every practice question you answered correctly.

Question # ___

- ☐ I understand why I chose the answer I chose.
- ☐ I chose the correct answer for the right reason.

Note: If you chose the right answer for the wrong reason, write out here why your reasoning was flawed:

____

____

____

Rules/concepts tested in this question and tips to remember this area of questioning in the future:

____

____

____

MCQ TIPS AND STRATEGIES

- If you have ruled out one or more answers and reviewed the facts and interrogatory and still don't know the correct answer, guess and return to this question at the end if you have time. You need to complete thirty-three questions per hour.
- Watch the time. Remember you must complete 50 questions in 90 minutes. Every half hour you should be completing about 17 questions. If you stick to this pace, you should finish on time.
- Have a guessing strategy. If you can't rule out any of the answer choices or if you run out of time, select a predetermined letter, such as C, and move on. If at ten minutes before the end of the session you are more than a few questions from finishing, implement your guessing strategy. Don't leave any questions blank.
- Be sure each response you mark in corresponds to the question you are actually answering. Due to exam day

nerves, it is easy to inadvertently answer on the wrong line. If you catch this early, you can fix it. So, every few questions, verify that you haven't skipped any questions or answers.

LAW SCHOOL ESSAYS

Even though the FYLSE no longer tests you on essays, you undoubtedly are still taking essay exams in law school. So, two points: first, it is worth really understanding how symbiotic they are—and that doing practice essays will still train your knowledge of the law. Second, seeing how essay strategies compare and contrast with MCQ strategies will help you become the MCQ Expert you need to be to pass the FYLSE.

Like MCQs, law school essays are made up of relatively short fact patterns. You must identify issues, state the applicable rules of law, logically apply the law you stated from memory to the given facts, and accordingly resolve the issues you identified in a way that comes to a reasoned conclusion, thereby answering the specific question or questions posed.

Critical reading is an indispensable skill for essays, just as for MCQs. Because you must produce an *organized* written product rather than just identify the best choice, you must also include time (during and after you read the interrogatory and facts) to *order* what you intend to say in a logical manner.

On essays, you must not only understand the rules and how they apply to the facts, but also to articulate those rules in your own words and analyze how the facts prove or disprove the elements of those rules. On MCQs, you must see those connections, but you don't have to write out anything yourself. When you write out practice essays, you are testing yourself on learning and being able to state rules of law in your own words. This is also why some people find essays more difficult. And, nonnative English speakers may have a tougher time with essays than with MCQs—yet another reason for additional practice both for law school and for the FYLSE.

We saw previously that MCQs have one correct or best answer choice; your mission is to seek and find it. On law school essays, you may not need to know the answer for certain. There may not even be one single answer to an essay question. Rather, the facts may provide a vehicle for you to give reasoned arguments as to how both sides would resolve the issues.

ESSAY-TEST TIPS AND STRATEGIES

The tips below focus on essay strategies for law school.

- Answer the questions asked and only the questions asked. Many students waste time on non-issues. Careless reading is often the culprit. Lawyers must be detailed.
- Approach essays as follows: (1) read the interrogatory and then read the facts. Then reread the interrogatory; (2) read every word using my three-sense technique, hearing, touch, and sight: read softly under your breath so you can hear yourself and touch each word as you read with your eyes.
- Slow down. Make certain *you* understand what is and what is not asked of you. Then, see how the facts fit the analytical steps of resolving the specific question or questions *before* you write your answer.
- Before you write, organize and outline. At a minimum, your outlining goal should be to note the main headings (and subheadings) you will include in your answer. There is often more than one logical way to organize. The best and easiest organization is usually to mirror the call of the question. But if the question is general or for some other reason you need another strategy, just be sure that you discuss the issues in some reasoned order, for example, you might organize a torts answer by party, lawsuit, or cause of action; a contract answer by communication or event; a criminal law essay by crime or by defendant where there are multiple defendants. Any systematic, logical organization is usually fine. Your outline is the framework for your organization, and your outline is often the first draft of headings that will serve as the graders' road map in your answer. Note that graders will judge you only on your answer, so writing an

elaborate outline that ends up in the trash will waste time. Include in your outline only what *you* need to write an organized answer.

- Determine how much time to spend on each call of the question if there is more than one interrogatory or if the interrogatory poses a multipart question. Make this determination by how complex each part is and how many facts relate to each part of the question. As you read the body of the question, put brackets around facts that relate to specific issues, and then arrows pointing back to the interrogatory asking about those issues. Generally, the more facts that relate to a particular call of the question, the more time you should spend writing on that call.
- Cross out words in the fact pattern after you write about the issues they raise in your answer. Then, look back at the fact pattern periodically to see if there are words you have not crossed out. Why are these facts states? What issues do they raise? Do they add to issues you have already analyzed?
- Use every fact the question gives you! This does not mean every word must be restated in your answer. (In fact, if you quote, do so selectively and use quotation marks.) It means you should *think about* each fact to see if it triggers an issue. Include it in your analysis if it supports or refutes some element of a rule of law, or otherwise affects some relevant argument.
- Write in plain, simple English that spells out your reasoning so clearly that even a non-lawyer could understand you!
- Focus on the most serious issues first (unless you are writing in another *logical* order, such as chronological order where appropriate). For example, if someone has battered a victim, and that victim dies as a result of the battery, start with the homicidal offenses before mentioning battery (if that is even relevant). Likewise, write about a

lesser included offense within the larger crime; for example, if there is a larceny and robbery, discuss a robbery first, and write about the larceny within the discussion of the robbery, since the larceny elements are "subsets" of the robbery elements.

Quick Test

What are the elements of robbery?

___

What are the elements of larceny?

___

- Write in complete sentences, thoroughly analyzing the facts to resolve the issues.
- Provide a key to any terms or party names that you abbreviate. For example, if you abbreviate "contract" with "K," write out "contract (K)" or "contract (hereinafter 'K')" the first time you use that abbreviation. You might think this association is so obvious that it's unnecessary to identify it, but the abbreviation "K" is also used to mean "$1,000," so even something so seemingly straightforward may be misconstrued.
- Avoid hammering on one point of view. Essays are about analysis not advocacy. Each issue may lend itself to both a defense and plaintiff/prosecution perspective, as the facts can and frequently do cut both ways. If you get stuck trying to advocate in a manner that's too one-sided, you may miss points to be gained from analyzing the opposing party's perspective. Note: If you write about two opposing arguments, conclude your thoughts by noting which side has the stronger position *and why* before moving on to your next area of discussion.
- Write complete (but succinct) rule statements, and then prove up (analyze) each element of each rule—piece by piece. Lawyers break complex thoughts down into logical parts. Elements are components

of the bundle that is a rule, and each part must be proved. This is also true for defenses, as defense theories often have multiple elements that must be discussed. (Always consider defenses when analyzing crimes or causes of action.) Know the difference between tests that include *factors* (all of which need not always be established) and *elements* (each of which must be proven by the requisite level of proof).

- Make sure your exams are reader friendly! Don't underestimate the importance of style. Am I suggesting form over substance? No! I am urging you to pay attention to form *in addition to* substance! The best essay answers tend to identify main areas of discussion with descriptive headings that provide a roadmap for graders to quickly see that the applicant identified the key issues and relevant rules. At a glance, the grader should be able to see that your answer is set out clearly and logically.

- Write using lawyerly language. I don't mean that you should use formal, ritualistic language ("the party of the first part heretofore contends . . ."). I mean that you should write in a clear and professional manner. Below are some examples I have seen frequently when students are concluding essays.

    - Do write: *For these reasons, the plaintiff is unlikely to prevail.* (Do **not** write: *The plaintiff's argument is really not going to fly.*)

    - Do write: *It is therefore possible for the plaintiff to prevail; however, for the reasons stated above, it appears that the defendant has the stronger argument here.* (Do **not** write: *This is a wash. It is up to the jury. The jurors could decide either way here.*)

- Avoid writing in the first person (do not use "I" or "we"). *Exam graders do not care what* you *think or what* you *believe*. What matters is whether the facts prove, or fail to prove, the particular legal theories you have articulated.

- Do write: *For the reasons stated above, the defendant will likely prevail.* (Do **not** write: *I think the defendant will win.*)
- Do write: *After weighing the facts on both sides and for the reasons stated above, it appears that the plaintiff has the stronger argument on this question because the plaintiff has more evidence and that evidence is more credible.* (Do **not** write: *I believe the plaintiff has the better argument.*)
- Do write: *The defendant's spitting on the plaintiff/victim is an offensive action. Reasonable people find spitting to be a rude and even demeaning gesture.* Do **not** write: *The defendant's spitting on the plaintiff/victim is an offensive action. I would be horrified if someone spat on me that way.*

READ YOUR ANSWERS ALOUD

I often ask students to read their practice test answers out loud. I do this in class and during office hours. Some students will read a paragraph and then stop themselves and say, "This doesn't make any sense." Or, "I'm not sure what I meant here." What you write must make sense to you if you want it to make sense to a grader. Reading answers aloud will help you see if what you wrote was logical, clear, and responsive.

MAKE SURE YOU CLOSE THE BOOKS

Students who do not do well on closed-book exams too often confess that they either never wrote closed-book practice tests at all, or only wrote them open book. Consequently, they never got their timing right and never memorized all the rules they needed to know. When you practice, force yourself to answer the questions under timed conditions, as fully as you can, without looking anything up, as if you were taking the actual exam. Only *after* you finish to the best of your ability should you study the sample or model answers, self-assess, and look up rules you do not know or understand.

LAW SCHOOL ESSAYS: A CLOSER LOOK AT HOW TO READ AND WRITE THEM

Start at the end of the fact pattern with the "call" of the question. That's what you must answer, so start there. Then read the fact pattern. Then reread the question. Read slowly and carefully, touching each word and mumbling it aloud under your breath, circling and highlighting key words.

Take notes. Jot down (on paper or start a "notes" section at the end of your draft answer file), noting any words that raise "discussable issues" (more on issue spotting below). As part of note-taking, you might want to also create a quick chronology, listing key facts in the order in which they occur. That can be especially helpful in certain subjects. For example, in a torts negligence fact pattern for which you are analyzing proximate cause, tracking the chain of causation requires knowing what happened and when. Essays often tell the factual "story" out of order. (Pay attention to dates.) Looking at your own ordered list of events on scratch paper or in a notes section of your draft answer, you will readily see if an event came between the defendant's actions and the victim's injury. You can then assess that intervening event to determine if it was foreseeable or not, and complete your proximate cause discussion. Another example is a contracts question in which there are numerous communications between the buyer and seller or between the employer and employee. In order to know the legal significance of each communication, you may need to know exactly what was communicated, and when (think "mailbox rule").

Next, create an outline. The best essay outlines are those that help you create a logical order without taking too much time, because most graders will not look at or consider your outline but only your completed answer. Think of your outline as a table of contents to your essay. Start by making sure your outline includes the main discussable issues and possibly relevant sub-issues, organized into a logical order (often, but not always, tracking the calls of the question). If you type your outline into your answer file, you can often turn your outline into headings in your actual answer. (Again, headings serve as a road map for graders.) For example, a question asks, "Of what crimes, if any, may the defendant be convicted?" Your headings may be each of the crimes you intend to discuss. Or, in a torts question involving multiple parties, the headings may be the various lawsuits: *A v. B*, *B v. C*, etc.

Remember: Before you upload your essays, delete any of your own internal notes and your draft outline.

LAW SCHOOL ESSAY WRITING IS LOGICAL WRITING

For law school essay writing, as I will detail below, I suggest using an approach similar to IRAC that I call IRPC—issue, rule, *proof*, conclusion.

When law students first hear about IRAC, they sometimes think it stands for "I Really Am Crazy" and wonder why they went to law school in the first place. But IRAC is just a tool—a template or system—to help students write logically.

IRAC forces the writer to move through steps (like A + B + C = D) and to remember to use the facts to prove or disprove the elements of the rules of law. In law school exams, as distinct from FYLSX or bar exams, the analysis portion is typically richer, deeper, and more thoughtful. On law school essays, you will want to weave into your analysis discussions of cases (with analogies and distinctions), policy concerns, and subtleties or relevant changes within the law itself, noting how those affect the resolution of the issues at hand. You may mention both majority and minority positions in evolving areas of law, or you may compare older case law to more modern trends you have studied. Of course, you must reason to a logical conclusion.

Let's look at the following example as a useful (albeit oversimplified) analogy for effective writing.

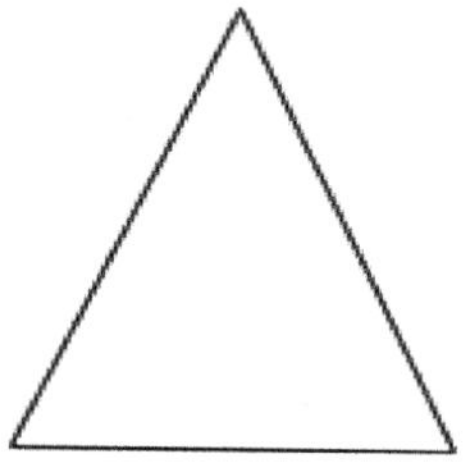

What sort of figure does the shape above represent? **[ISSUE]**

Three-sided figures with sides coming together at three corners are generally known as *triangles*. An equilateral triangle is a three-sided figure in which all three sides are equal in length and all corners have the same degree angle. **[RULE]**

Here, side A measures *x* inches, side B measures *x* inches, and side C measures *x* inches. The three sides are touching and meet at three corners. Each angle measures *y* degrees. **[PROOF** (or analysis)**]**

Therefore, the figure represented above is an equilateral triangle. **[CONCLUSION]**

This logic may sound more mathematical than legal, but it is highly instructive. Let's consider another IRPC example, this one using an everyday driving scenario in which you will see the same sort of logic but in a situation that more closely resembles a law-type fact pattern.

> The defendant and his passenger, Witness X, both testified that the defendant's car was in the left-turn lane, the green arrow was blinking, and it was 3:00 p.m. when the turn was made. Did the defendant's turn from Elm Street onto Main Street on December 1 violate traffic regulations?

Now let's say you know (because you have learned the relevant rule of law) that left turns are permitted from the left-turn lane at the intersection of Elm and Main when the green left-turn arrow is blinking at times other than 4:00 to 7:00 p.m. on weekdays. (From 4:00 p.m. to 7:00 p.m. on weekdays, such turns are not permitted even if the arrow is green.) Now, using an "IRPC" format, how would we logically deconstruct the legality of the turn in question?

Did the defendant's 3:00 p.m. left turn at Elm and Main violate traffic laws with respect to turning? **[ISSUE]**

Left turns are permitted at the intersection of Elm and Main from the left-turn lane when the green left-t urn arrow is blinking and at times other than between 4:00 and 7:00 p.m. on weekdays. **[RULE]**

The defendant was in the left-t urn lane (the proper location to make a left turn). He saw the turn arrow blinking (the signal that it was safe to make his turn). The defendant made the turn in question at 3:00 p.m. (an appropriate time for this type of turn). Since it was 3:00 p.m., it did not matter which day of the week it was, as the only restrictions on turning are from 4:00 to 7:00 p.m. **[PROOF or analysis]**

Last but not least, policy would dictate that even if the defendant had followed the technical requirements for turning, he must have also confirmed that it was generally safe to make the turn—t hat is, that there were no other obstacles, emergency vehicles, or unanticipated conditions that would make the turn unsafe. Assuming the defendant did confirm this, there is no indication that the turn was unlawful. **[NOTE: This paragraph weaves in POLICY**—as an optional, bonus point issue.]

Therefore, the defendant's turn from Elm onto Main appears to have been lawful. **[CONCLUSION]**

This is straightforward, right? It makes sense. It is not mysterious or intriguing. It is not eloquent. It is simple and direct, logical and organized.

CRITICAL READING AND ITS RELATIONSHIP TO CRITICAL WRITING

Both to issue spot and to prove your points, you must read carefully, *and think*, as you read. Let's look at a couple of examples in the context of criminal law. Criminal law fact patterns often include one or more defendants who will have done a series of actions that arguably amount to criminal offenses. You must *use* the facts to demonstrate the proof or lack thereof of the requisite conduct, mental state, or any other elements of those crimes, and to demonstrate which, if any, defenses apply.

As we have discussed, start with the call of the question, or interrogatory (often presented at the end of the fact pattern). This way, you immediately discern what the question is asking so that you can answer that question or questions—and *only* that question or questions.

The interrogatory in a criminal law essay may ask something like this: *With what crime or crimes, if any, may the defendant be charged?* or *Of what crime or crimes may the defendant be found guilty?* or *Did the court err in convicting the defendant of any crime or crimes?* By reading the interrogatory first, you will know just a moment into the exam that you are dealing with criminal law.

Exam questions will not be labeled by subject, so the very first step to take in approaching an essay or multiple choice question is to determine whether it is torts, contracts, or criminal law, and then "call up" (on your *mental* thumb drive) the relevant rules while you read the facts.

After reading the interrogatory, go to the top of the page and read the entire fact pattern, slowly and carefully. Use the active reading techniques discussed earlier. Read simultaneously with three senses: touch, hearing, and sight. Put your finger, pen, or stylus on each word as you read it with your eyes and say it in a barely audible voice. Circle, underline, highlight, and write notes on or near words that seem significant. If a word or phrase triggers an issue or leads you to see a point you might want to discuss in your writing, note it right away so you do not forget. Mark directly on the question using online annotation tools, jot your thoughts on scratch paper, or type right into the document that may start as your outline and then become your essay answer. (If your outline is made up of your headings, then you can simply type each section under the appropriate heading.)

Let's practice with the following short essay question:

> Defendant wanted to burn Vicki's cottage. Defendant walked to the cottage, carrying matches and kerosene, and lit a match, setting fire to a chair in the living room. A neighbor smelled smoke and called the fire department. Firefighters came within moments and extinguished the flaming chair. Of what crime or crimes may Defendant be convicted?

What did you read first? Hopefully, the last sentence, "Of what crime or crimes may Defendant be convicted?" That reveals critical information, that you are being tested on criminal law. Next, read the short fact pattern. "Burn" is a trigger term for a criminal law question. What crime do you think of when you heard the word burn? The minute you saw the word *burn*, you might have recited the definition of arson in your mind and asked yourself, *Do these facts prove that the defendant committed arson?*

The common law definition of *arson* is the malicious burning of the dwelling house of another. Modern variations relax some of the traditional elements. For example, modern jurisdictions have extended arson to include most any protected structure, not just a "dwelling," and a defendant can, in certain circumstances, be convicted of arson for burning his or her own house down, not just the property "of another."

You might not have every rule memorized yet, but you must have all the main rules committed to memory by the time of your exam. Knowing the rules is necessary to effectively issue spot. All the relevant crimes, causes of action, defense theories, and other testable principles must be as accessible to you during your exam as the passwords you use every day. The applicable rules must be memorized succinctly enough that you can spit them out quickly on essays. If you see the word *burn* in a criminal law fact pattern, you want to automatically recite the elements of arson, and then read and think through the facts *with that definition in mind.*

Note: be thorough but directed in your rule statements. You will not get "extra credit" for knowing and listing all the exceptions to a rule, for example, if those exceptions do not apply to the facts at hand.

Back to arson—back to the fact pattern and to what you were thinking as you read. (I'll paraphrase your potential thoughts in italics.) For this example, we'll use the common law definition of *arson*: again, the malicious burning of the dwelling house of another.

> With what crime or crimes may Defendant be convicted? (*OK, I'm in criminal law, so I'll think about possible crimes as I read.*) Defendant **wanted to burn** (*Defendant's desire to burn the cottage proves his willful intent and satisfies the malice or* mens rea *element of arson*) Vicki's cottage (*the dwelling of another*). Defendant walked to the cottage, carrying matches and kerosene, and lit a match, setting fire to a chair in the living room. A neighbor smelled smoke and called the fire department. Firefighters came within moments and extinguished the flaming chair. (*The chair was flaming, but did the flames burn or char any part of the structure itself?*) Of what crime or crimes may Defendant be convicted?

"Issue spotting," and what that really means, can confuse people. Start by thinking of issue spotting as looking for those places where the facts raise *questions* about whether or not an element of a crime, cause of action, or defense has been or can be proven. One expert suggests that after reading the facts, students think about and develop theories based on those facts from one side's perspective. Then "switch hats." Put yourself in the mindset of opposing counsel and look to expose any weaknesses in the arguments you just thought of. Those weaknesses form the basis of many of the issues you should discuss in your answer.

But some of what you must write in essays relates to what appear to be non-issues. In other words, you must state whether or not each element was established under these facts and why, even an element that does not seem to be in question. For example, in the arson question above, the facts say that Defendant "wanted to burn." It therefore seems wholly obvious that the defendant possessed the requisite *intent* for arson. But you still have to *prove* he had the requisite intent. Here you might do that by simply referring in your answer to his "wanting" to burn the structure as evidence of his intent. (See sample answers below.)

Reading further, you will notice that from the information we are given, it appears that only *the chair* burned, not the structure. So, you will have to use the facts given to determine whether there was a requisite burning to support an arson conviction. (That's issue spotting.)

Once you read carefully and issue spot, you can start making an outline. Take a moment and write an outline of the Defendant arson hypothetical in the spaces below, and then consider the sample outline.

Essay Outline

Draft an outline of the crime or crimes for which Defendant may be convicted here below.

CRIMES OF DEFENDANT

ARSON?

a. Malicious? (wanted to burn = willful, so yes)

b. Burning? (the chair burned; need to demonstrate charring or burning of structure, as smoke damage is not enough, so no), of the

c. Dwelling house? (cottage, yes)

d. Of another? (Vicki's cottage, so yes)

Would you be done if you concluded (which you should, after discussing *all* the elements of arson) that Defendant will *not* likely be convicted of arson? No. Remember that the question being asked is: "Of what crime or *crimes may* Defendant be convicted?" You need to discuss *any and all* of the relevant crimes.

So what should you ask yourself now? You know this! Whether Defendant might be guilty of *attempted arson*. To determine that, you have to resolve yet another issue: whether Defendant's action of setting fire to the chair was sufficiently close to the completed offense to find him guilty of an attempted crime. To reason to a logical conclusion on that point, you must know the rule or test for attempt in your jurisdiction. (There are several, including those that look at whether the defendant "took a substantial step toward" or was in "dangerous proximity of" completing the offense and those that consider whether the defendant did the "last act" before actually completing the target offense tested. The outcome may differ depending on the test used.)

Let's continue our outline then, adding this second possible crime.

CRIMES OF DEFENDANT SAMPLE OUTLINE CONTINUED

ATTEMPTED ARSON?

a. Acting with specific intent to burn the structure in question? (wanted to burn, yes)

b. Defendant took a substantial step toward completing this arson? (Yes, Defendant "walked to" the cottage, carrying matches and kerosene, a highly flammable liquid, and lit a match, setting fire to a chair in the living room).

Are you done now? *Well, wait a minute!* you say. *If the chair burned, then didn't Defendant permanently deprive Vicki of her property? Surely she didn't consent to that. Should I discuss larceny?* You quickly rattle off the elements of larceny: "the trespassory taking and carrying away of the personal property of another with intent to deprive the owner thereof," and you continue thinking, *Ah, but he didn't move the chair at all.*

Let's finish off the sample outline.

LARCENY?

a. Taking and carrying away? (no, the movement or asportation element of larceny is not satisfied here)

b. Of personal property of another? (yes, Vicki's chair)

c. With intent to permanent deprive? (unclear)

OK, we read carefully. We *thought* as we read, asking ourselves questions about what was potentially in question or at issue while looking at each word. We took notes so as not to lose those thoughts. Then we outlined, placing the points we want to write about in a logical order. Now let's translate this into exam writing.

Note: This is a sample only, using a truncated hypothetical. You may not have time to or need to go into this much detail. This would likely be only one paragraph in a longer fact pattern, and there would be many other main issues or sub-issues to discuss. But this short sample gives you an idea of how to read, think, and write essays, hitting each part of IRPC and making your reasoning explicit enough for a layperson to easily follow your thinking.

WRITING EXAMPLE #1

Crimes of Defendant

The defendant may be charged with several crimes, but under these facts there is only one crime of which he may likely be convicted. [This is an optional sort of introduction. It shows the grader you read the question and are planning to respond to it. You might write this when you finish and insert it here at the beginning if time permits.]

ARSON

Will Defendant be convicted of arson? Arson is the malicious burning of the dwelling house of another. ("Malice" can be proved by establishing either willfulness or a reckless disregard for the risks.) Here, the facts state that Defendant "wanted" to burn Vicki's cottage and that he "walked to" the cottage with matches and kerosene (the tools necessary to set a fire). His desire to burn the cottage and his going to the target site with those tools prove that Defendant acted deliberately or willfully, therefore establishing "malice" and satisfying *the mens rea requirement for arson.* A cottage is typically a *dwelling house*, and this cottage belongs to Vicki; therefore, it would be the dwelling house of another and satisfy the *structure requirement* of common law arson. The *burning element* of arson, however, would not likely be satisfied here since that requires some burning or charring of the structure itself. Here the flames appear to have been extinguished while only the chair was burning—before the fire could reach the floor, walls, or any other part of the structure. Assuming that is the case and no part of the structure actually burned or was charred, despite the fact that Defendant possessed the requisite intent and took some action toward committing the crime, *Defendant may not be convicted of arson.*

ATTEMPTED ARSON

Will Defendant be guilty of attempted arson? A conviction of attempted arson here would require proof of Defendant's *specific intent to burn* Vicki's home, and evidence that Defendant *took a substantial step toward the completion* of that crime. Here, as was noted in the discussion of arson above, the defendant "wanted" to burn Vicki's cottage. His specific intent is evidenced by that fact. Next, Defendant "walked to" the cottage, with "kerosene" (a highly flammable liquid) and "matches" (incendiary devices), went to Vicki's cottage (her dwelling place), and lit a chair on fire inside the home. These actions go far beyond merely thinking about committing the offense or even simply *planning* to burn the cottage. The defendant went to the site where he wanted to commit the target offense and started a fire in the home, an action very likely to have led to the burning of the cottage had the neighbor and fire department not intervened so quickly. The defendant was thus well beyond the zone of preparation and well within the *zone of perpetration*. Because the prosecution has ample evidence of both the specific intent to complete the arson and his having taken a substantial step toward completing that act, *Defendant will likely be convicted of attempted arson.*

LARCENY

Did Defendant's actions in deliberately setting fire to Vicki's chair amount to a larceny? Larceny is the taking and carrying away of the personal property of another with intent to permanently deprive the owner thereof. Defendant may have deprived Vicki of her chair (a moveable object and thus personal property), and done so intentionally, but nowhere do the facts tell us that Defendant took or carried the chair away. Because Defendant did not move the chair, the asportation element of larceny is not satisfied, and *Defendant will not be convicted of larceny*.

CONCLUSION

For the reasons stated above, and because the facts do not appear to raise any plausible defense theories, Defendant will likely be convicted of attempted arson, but not convicted of arson or larceny.

Notice how the writing sample above tracks the logic of IRPC and is written in complete sentences in a way that a layperson could understand and follow the reasoning. In the example above, we *italicized* elements and conclusions to provide a road map for the grader. It would also be possible to set the same answer up with subheadings, as in the example below.

WRITING EXAMPLE #2

This answers the same question but using a slightly differently style, with shorter paragraphs and more frequent headings and subheadings. Neither is "right." As you read, think about which you prefer.

Crimes of Defendant

The defendant may be charged with several crimes, but under these facts there is only one crime of which he may likely be convicted.

ARSON

Will Defendant be convicted of arson, the malicious burning of the dwelling house of another?

Malice or mens rea requirement

("Malice" can be proved by either establishing willfulness or a reckless disregard for the risks.) Here, the facts state that Defendant "wanted" to burn Vicki's cottage and that he "walked to" the cottage with the tools to do so. His desire to burn the cottage and his going to the target site with those tools prove that Defendant acted deliberately or willfully, therefore establishing "malice" and satisfying the mens rea requirement for arson.

Dwelling house of another

A cottage is typically a place people live (so qualifies as a dwelling house), and this cottage belongs to Vicki; therefore, it would satisfy the structure requirement of common law arson, the dwelling house of another.

Burning

The burning element of arson, however, would not likely be satisfied here. This element requires some burning or charring of the structure itself, and the flames appear to have been extinguished while only the chair was burning—before the fire could reach the floor, walls, or any other part of the structure.

Assuming that is the case and no part of the structure actually burned or was charred, despite the fact that Defendant possessed the requisite intent and took some action toward committing the crime, he may not be convicted of arson.

ATTEMPTED ARSON

Will Defendant be guilty of attempted arson? A conviction of attempted arson here would require proof of Defendant's specific intent to burn Vicki's home, as well as evidence that Defendant took a substantial step toward the completion of that crime such that he crossed over from what might be deemed merely the "zone of preparation" into the "zone of perpetration."

Mens rea: specific intent to complete the target offense

Here, as was noted in the previous discussion of arson, the defendant "wanted" to burn Vicki's cottage. His specific intent to complete the target offense is evidenced by that fact.

Actus reus: the defendant took a substantial step toward completing the crime

One test used to evidence a "substantial step" is where the defendant's actions are said to move beyond the zone of preparation and into the zone of perpetration.

Here, Defendant "walked to" the cottage with "kerosene" (a highly flammable liquid) and "matches" (incendiary devices), went to Vicki's home, and lit a chair inside the home on fire. These actions go far beyond thinking about committing the offense or even simply *planning* to burn the cottage. The defendant went to the site where he wanted to commit the target offense and started a fire in the home, an action very likely to have led to the burning of the cottage had the neighbor and fire department not intervened so quickly. The defendant was thus well within the "zone of perpetration."

Because the prosecution has ample evidence of both the specific intent to complete the arson and his having taken a substantial step toward completing that act, Defendant will likely be convicted of attempted arson.

LARCENY

Did Defendant's actions in deliberately setting fire to Vicki's chair amount to a larceny? Larceny is the taking and carrying away of the personal property of another with intent to permanently deprive the owner thereof. Defendant may have deprived Vicki of her chair (a moveable good and her personal property), and done so intentionally, but nowhere do the facts tell us that Defendant took, carried, or even moved the chair. Because Defendant did not move the chair, the carrying away or asportation element of larceny is not satisfied, and Defendant will not be convicted of larceny.

DEFENSES

The facts do not appear to raise any justification or excuse for Defendant' actions, nor are there any mitigating factors.

CONCLUSION

For the reasons stated above, Defendant will likely be convicted of attempted arson; however, Defendant will not be convicted of arson or larceny.

Notice in this second example that there was no need to *italicize* key terms because the headings and subheadings gave the grader a clear road map. The purpose of these basic examples was to take you through the process, from critical reading, thinking and issue spotting, to outlining, and then writing simply in a logical *IRPC* style, proving each element of the rules you stated with facts from the fact pattern.

LAW SCHOOL ESSAYS: PROVE IT, DON'T ASSUME IT

You must explicitly state all of the steps in your logic, even points that may seem obvious. In the Defendant example above, the facts convey that Defendant "wanted to burn" the cottage. How much more obvious could his intent be? It is clearly stated. Nonetheless, in your answer, you must state that the intent element was proved and why—even if that "why" is because the facts stated that "he wanted to burn."

Let's say you read a fact pattern and determine that the main crime the defendant may have committed is burglary. (First, of course, you would recite the rule, "At common law, a burglary was the breaking and entering of the dwelling house of another in the nighttime with intent to commit a felony therein.") One element of burglary is *breaking* into the structure. Even when a fact pattern explicitly states that the defendant "broke the door to go inside," you would need to say something to briefly indicate that the facts prove the existence of that element. For example, you might write, *The breaking element is satisfied here because the facts state that the defendant "broke the door" to go inside.* While that may seem self-evident, points are often given on essays for stating the obvious in a clear and organized fashion. This shows that you see the relevance of the particular facts and can apply the facts to that law. (This is precisely how litigators help jurors see how evidence presented at trial proves or disproves elements of the causes of action or crimes in question.)

What you do not want to do is *assume*, here meaning to arrive at a conclusion without saying why and making your reasoning explicit. That is what law professors and exam graders call *conclusory*. (Jurors may not convict a defendant without believing beyond a reasonable doubt that there is sufficient evidence of each and every element of the charged crime, right?) Let's look back at the example of Defendant's attempted arson above. We did not just write, *Defendant wanted to burn the cottage and took a substantial step toward doing so and therefore is guilty of attempt*. We broke down each element (the intent element was easy to prove because the facts stated he wanted to do this, but we nonetheless still noted it explicitly) and then showed how and *why* Defendant's walking to the cottage with the kerosene and matches (linking these tools explicitly to the target offense) amounts to a substantial step toward the commission of the crime.

You may think this is obvious, so why bother writing it? Of *course* kerosene is flammable. On an essay, though, your job is *to show why* the facts prove or disprove the elements of the relevant rules. The most important thing is the *Why?* You must always explain your reasoning and make your thoughts explicit. (And picturing yourself writing to a non-lawyer rather than to a professor will also help you to note every step of your reasoning more clearly.)

Issue-Spotting Exercise

Look at the following sentence: "The defendant entered the Miller office building at dusk through an unlocked door to get the umbrella that he had left, then saw the diamond ring, took it, and walked out into the rain." If the question asks about the defendant's possible criminal liability for burglary, what, if any, discussable issues are raised by the following words? Write your thoughts about these words in the spaces below:

"office building at dusk"

"through an unlocked door"

"that he had left"

"then"

What did you identify as issues? Before identifying any issues, of course, you recited the rule: *Common law burglary is defined as the breaking and entering into the dwelling house of another in the nighttime with intent to commit a felony therein.* **(Note: if you did not know the rule, you could not effectively issue spot.)** Then you perhaps went on to ask some of the following questions:

1. Does the office building satisfy the "dwelling house" element of burglary? (Here, you likely reminded yourself that modern jurisdictions have extended this element to include any "protected structure.")

2. And, do the words "at dusk" satisfy the "in the nighttime" element? Again, this element has been eliminated under modern law.
3. Does entering through an unlocked door satisfy the "breaking" element?
4. Is the defendant's going inside to get the umbrella "that he had left" sufficient to prove he had the requisite *mens rea*, or "intent to commit a felony therein"? He may not have had any criminal intent if he walked in to retrieve his own property.
5. Does the word "then" raise a potential issue? It may be relevant to the question of when the felonious intent was formed, timing being critical to culpability.

I hope this one sentence issue spotting exercise illustrates how both knowledge of the law, and slow, careful reading are indispensable to effective issue spotting.

CONCLUSIONS IN ESSAY ANSWERS

Finally, a word about conclusions. While it may not always matter so much *how* you conclude or "who wins" on essays, it matters that you do conclude. Graders (usually your professors) want to see that you can answer the entire question (and all of the issues that it raises) within the allotted time. They will not be satisfied if you merely demonstrate that you can *start* answering the questions or outline the answers to the questions. But two passing answers may contain opposite conclusions—especially when the facts are "gray," meaning there are good arguments on both sides. When faced with such ambiguity, you may, for instance, conclude in a manner that acknowledges this: *Based on the foregoing analysis, the defendant will* likely *be found to have possessed the intent to kill the victim here. If, however, the prosecution is unable to prove intent to kill, also as noted above, the prosecution may well be able to demonstrate that the defendant possessed the intent to cause serious bodily harm or, at the very least, that his actions showed a reckless indifference to human life.* On most exam questions, there is typically nothing wrong with concluding in a way that shows a number of probable outcomes, but you must finish and do so logically. Again, giving some emphasis to a conclusion, even a brief one (perhaps by underlining it or making it a subheading), shows the grader that you completed the answer.

Quick Quiz

TEST YOUR HABITS: When I complete a practice exam, I:

A. Never look at it again, and certainly never show it to anyone else.

B. Study it alongside a sample or model answer, comparing and contrasting the two.

C. Show it to a professor, mentor, or study buddy to review and critique.

D. Do either *B* or *C*, or both, *and* rewrite that same practice exam at a later date and assess improvements.

Many of you, if you are honest, will choose *A*. Hopefully, I will have convinced you to choose D after completing a practice exam. If you picked *B*, that is good; however, be sure at some point to also have someone else critique at least some of your exams, hopefully early on, so that you are not mistakenly thinking your answers are just fine if they aren't. There is also a danger in not studying reliable sample or model answers; you risk cementing your errors and continuing to repeat the same mistakes. The goal is to improve with every practice exam. You do yourself the greatest of disservices if you simply compound your mistakes. That said, if you picked *C*, be sure in the future to *first try to figure out* what *you* think you missed, and *then* let someone else critique it. Hopefully, what they say mirrors what you saw as errors and ways to improve. Eventually, you will learn what you need to from studying reliable sample or model answers on your own. (After all, you will not have someone critiquing or editing your actual exam answers. You must get to the point where you are doing them well, alone, but it is a process getting there! And, reality checks along the way are important.)

HOW TO SELF-ASSESS YOUR PRACTICE ESSAY WRITING TO IMPROVE IN LAW SCHOOL

Right after completing a practice essay, look carefully at your own answer and a model or reliable sample answer. Sit with both. How are they the same and how do they differ? Pay attention to content, organization, phrasing, and presentation. Note how precise and complete the rule statements are. Are there any rules you can learn more about or rule statements you can memorize more thoroughly? What about proof (application/analysis)? Is there proof of the existence or lack thereof of each element of each rule at issue? Was every key fact used? Review them side by side, and, as a clever detective:

- look for what the sample or model answers include that your answer did not contain, and what you may have written about that was not in the sample answers;
- be sure you understand *why* the sample answers included what was discussed and why the sample answers left out things you may have thought were important;
- look for content, organization, and style (make sure your answer is reader friendly!);
- look at the rules and be sure you understand them; and
- reread the fact pattern and then look at how the facts were used in discussing each issue in the model answer.

Then, after this basic compare-and-contrast, ask these specific questions and check the appropriate boxes:

- ☐ Did I finish within the allotted time?
- ☐ Did I spot the main discussable issues? (And did I see which issues were major and required more discussion, and which were minor and called for less emphasis?)
- ☐ Did I state the rules correctly and succinctly?
- ☐ Did I use facts to show why (to *prove*) each element of each rule was or was not established in the question?
- ☐ Did I reason to a logical conclusion for every main issue I raised?
- ☐ Was my answer presented in a manner that was organized and easy to read?

After you have done this first part of self-assessing, find concrete ways to improve. The examples below are illustrations. Your situation is unique to you. The key is to figure out where you need to improve and to then create a doable plan of action for your success. Make every effort to leave each practice session with at least two to three specific ideas about how you can improve.

> CAVEAT: USE PRACTICE EXAMS TO IMPROVE!
>
> I have said this before but cannot emphasize it enough: *taking* practice exams is not sufficient. You must walk away from every practice session dedicated to *improving* the quality of what you just produced. If you write essays poorly, you get the law wrong or your analysis (proof) or use of the facts is insufficient, or your answer is disorganized—and you just keep repeating the same mistakes on future practice exams—you will just be cementing and compounding your weaknesses. That is why you must study quality, reliable answers and learn how to make your answers look and read more like those passing answers. This is also why it can be so helpful to at least periodically have your answers reviewed and critiqued by someone reliable.

ACTION ITEMS FOR IMPROVEMENT IN LAW SCHOOL ESSAY WRITING

Check those items that apply to you.

- ☐ I must read the questions more carefully. (Note a specific example of something you did not read carefully enough, for instance, "I wrote about other crimes but the call of the question specifically asked about homicidal offenses.") In upcoming exams, I will read the call of the question first, then read the facts, and then reread the call of the question before I begin outlining. I will also underline the call of the question, and I will keep the fact pattern and my outline in front of me as I write my answer.
- ☐ I need to manage my time better. I will work on my timing. During a one-hour essay, for example, I will note when I reach the fifteen, thirty, forty-five, and fifty-five-minute marks. I will try to finish my outline in the first 15 minutes. I will strive to have

hit all the main issues by 45 minutes. And, I will be concluding by 55 minutes, leaving me 5 minutes to proofread.

> A NOTE ON TIMING
>
> It is critical to have your timing down. You must go into your law school exams knowing you can answer them within the allotted time frames. And, for the Baby Bar, you must take the exam knowing you can read each MCQ question and select the best answer within 1.8 minutes.

- ☐ I must type faster. (I have the thoughts in my head, but don't get them out fast enough.) I will work on improving my typing skills.
- ☐ I need to understand the law better. (I either did not see issues or I saw what the issues were but did not write applicable rule statements clearly.) I will review the lecture notes and look up areas I do not understand in the outlines. Then I will either say out loud or copy or rewrite the legal rules several times to help memorize them.
- ☐ I'm not using enough facts. Cross out words from the fact pattern as you use them in your answer. Learn the law more thoroughly. The better your knowledge of the law, the better your ability to quickly see how these new facts prove or disprove elements of governing rules.

Your Turn to Self-Assess

1. Did I finish the entire practice essay within the allotted time? ☐ Yes ☐ No

Improvement action:

____

2. Did I spot and write about the main issues? ☐ Yes ☐ No
Improvement action:

3. Did I allocate my time well as I was writing? (Did I write too much on any one issue such that I gave short shrift to other issues?) ☐ Yes ☐ No
Improvement action:

4. Did I state the rules correctly and succinctly? ☐ Yes ☐ No
Improvement action:

5. Did I use facts to show why each element of each rule was or was not established in the question? ☐ Yes ☐ No
Improvement action:

6. Did I reason to a logical conclusion for every main issue I raised? ☐ Yes ☐ No
Improvement action:

7. Was my answer presented in a manner that was organized and easy to read? ☐ Yes ☐ No
Improvement action:

Bottom line: practicing MCQs is essential for success on the Baby Bar, and practicing all testing formats will be essential for law school and bar exam success after graduation. And, taking practice exams builds transferable skills. Practicing with essays can help you learn the law you need to know for MCQs and vice versa. The more practice exams you take, the more opportunities you will have to learn and improve, slowly and surely. Every practice test is an investment in you. Don't miss out on these opportunities to invest in your future success!

CHAPTER 7

THE HOME STRETCH: ELIMINATE DISTRACTIONS AND EMBRACE SUCCESS

CHAPTER SUMMARY: This Chapter sets out strategies for success in the final timeline before your FYLSX.

The saying "It's always darkest before the dawn" applies to the home stretch before the exam. This chapter gives you tools to keep going, even when you feel you cannot. It will help you see that you are almost there and stay the course.

- Combat burnout. You may feel fried. If you have put in a tough year of law school and now this exam on top of it is even tougher.
- Pace yourself. Before the exam, take care of some business. Make sure that all the logistics are handled.
- Don't forget self-care, sleep, exercise, and eating healthy foods. Being strong is just as important as memorizing rules. At the actual exam, someone else may know more law than you. No matter how much you study, that is possible. But, when all is said and done, if that person is too tired to be an active, detail-oriented reader, all the memorized rules in the world won't help.

  Yes, you must know your stuff. But you must also go in pumped up and ready to read critically, understand every word of every question, and use that information to think and reason carefully to logical conclusions, finding the best answer choices. The facts will be new to every applicant, and the person who stayed up all night before the exam to pack in more rules may not be awake and alert enough to read the facts critically and intelligently answer the questions asked.

- Take a full simulated exam—look at it not as a referendum on how you will do on the real exam, but as a learning tool. Work on improving wherever you still need to.
- Draft 1 page "cheat sheets" for each of the three tested subjects.
- Be good to yourself. Sleep well, eat well, exercise regularly, and get ready for battle.

ELIMINATE DISTRACTIONS AND FOCUS FULLY

When you started preparing for the exam, you worked to *reduce* distractions; when you are closing in on your goal, *eliminate* them. As the exam approaches, shut virtually everything down. Until it's over, give this exam your single-minded, total focus. Total immersion.

During the home stretch, you must cocoon. In those last weeks and days, it must be all FYLSX, all the time. Learn to be "self-centered" in a good way, in a way that allows for success.

This is a huge challenge. It is not easy, but it is wholly doable. Do not feel weak because you are nervous. Fear can be a good thing! It can be power, especially if you use it productively.

"Courage is resistance to fear, mastery of fear—not absence of fear."

—MARK TWAIN—

SIMULATED EXAMS AS THE "DRESS REHEARSAL"

Make a few simulated exams part of your plan—days where you complete 100 MCQs in all three subjects mixed up randomly. Taking at least one simulated exam can give you a much-needed reality check. If you identify weak areas, study those. You can see what times of day you have the most energy and when you are dragging. The real exam will seem less daunting after making it through a trial run. You gain the confidence to believe that you can intelligently reason through anything they throw at you.

DON'T LET YOUR SIMULATED EXAM FREAK YOU OUT

Do not get discouraged. Simulated exams help you when they provide an opportunity to make necessary adjustments before the real thing. For many reasons, however, simulated exams are *not* necessarily a referendum on how you will actually perform on the exam. They are an opportunity to get lots of useful information. Use that data wisely. Use the time left to improve! Consider the following:

- You don't have to take the real thing today. It's still some time away. (It may not feel like a lot of time—but think about how much you were able to learn in one day before certain finals! There is still a lot you can clarify.)
- Your simulated exam may have been harder than the real exam.
- The real thing is a pass/fail test; you don't have to get an A.
- The simulated exam can help you strategize ways to plan the actual exam to maximize energy and efficiency.

Simulated FYLSX

After completing a simulated exam, ask the following questions:

Did you budget your time well? Did you spend 1.8 minutes per MCQ? Did you go over time? Did you speed through, finish early, and miss a number of questions? Note your thoughts and observations—points you want to remind yourself about timing:

Were you tired? What foods did you eat before the exam? How much did you eat? Note your thoughts on food and fatigue:

Did you "blank out" on any questions? If so, get a plan ready to work through a temporary "brain freeze" should one occur during the actual exam.

Were there any sub-topics you dreaded? (Maybe you were comfortable with homicidal offenses but not so much with theft crimes, for example.) Look at those again now. Try not to go in with an exposed weakness. Note your thoughts on areas you still want to review:

THE DAYS BEFORE THE EXAM: GETTING READY

- Review your condensed outlines—the one-page "cheat sheets" we talked about earlier that you prepared for all three subjects. Put any big books or outlines you are using on the shelf. No more reading long outlines. No time left to do that.

- Memorize rules. You have been memorizing slowly and surely for months. Now is the time for your final push. Aim for instant recall of all key rules.
- Read some of the practice MCQs aloud.
- Don't let anything faze you. It's all about the exam and you. Keep your own head clear. Stay *calm, confident, and in control* (your "three Cs" on exam days.)
- Keep your daily routine. Drink your coffee, tea, hot water, or whatever you have when you wake up just like you do every day. Continue to exercise. Eat healthy meals at regular times.
- In the days before the exam, if you cannot focus on any sort of review or study, then exercise, eat well, and sleep. Or watch a movie! Do whatever will get your body and mind ready for peak performance.

NO ONE ELSE KNOWS WHAT'S RIGHT
FOR YOU BEFORE THE EXAM

Some people will say study the day before the exam. Others will say, "Whatever you do, do not study." It does not matter what others say. It's *your* exam. Do what works for *you*.

The exam is your time push off and soar to success. Like a high diver, you may feel fear when poised to jump, but you will also feel excitement and empowerment. You are ready to go. Sure, it's scary. It's supposed to be. But this is your moment.

Some things to remember when you go in: If you love puzzles, think of the fact patterns that will be placed before you as puzzles. Every fact in every MCQ is there for you; you just have to connect the dots.

If you are more of a people person than a puzzle person, read your exam questions as if they were real people's stories. In your mind are the rules that help unravel how each of those stories can play out. Feel the incredible power that comes with knowing you can do that unraveling. You can and will pick each fact pattern and each answer choice apart and decide based on logic and knowledge of the law which answer choice is best.

Take in and appreciate the feeling of richness that comes from having so many rules at your command. It's like being ready to run a marathon knowing that all your muscles are strong. The intellectual flab has melted away through the long hours of mental work out. All the rules you need will be packed into your memory in a usable place, ready to be called upon.

Appreciate how strong you are. When exam day approaches, go in strong despite the fears. Muster as much confidence as you can. You are ready.

TOP TEN TEST-TAKING TIPS: MCQs

1. Read the facts and interrogatory carefully.

2. Read the answer choices carefully. Read with your finger, your eyes, and your voice at the same time. Touch the screen.

3. Try to first reason through to the correct answer from reading the interrogatory and facts without looking at the answer choices. Then proceed to the answer choices.

4. Look for and cross out answer choices that have internally incorrect or inconsistent statements.

5. Look for and cross out answer choices that don't answer the question asked.

6. If a question is stumping you, stay calm. You don't have to get 100%.

7. If you must guess, eliminate any answer choices you can, then guess from the remaining answers. Have a system to keep track of guesses so that you can come back to them if you finish early and have extra time.

8. Watch the time and stay on pace.

9. When you are close to the end, guess on any questions you know you won't get to. Don't leave any blank.

10. Breathe and stay as calm as possible throughout the whole exam.

CHAPTER 8

CELEBRATE YOUR ACHIEVEMENT AND ACKNOWLEDGE AND THANK THOSE WHO HELPED YOU (THEN SET YOUR NEXT GOAL!)

In the weeks before the exam, plan as if you have passed. This sounds silly; after all, you don't *know* yet that you passed. But it is really important to validate your hard work and acknowledge the support of those who helped you!

Plan ahead so that a special celebration awaits after you finish the exam. It will keep you motivated, and it will keep family or significant other on board. It gives everyone something to look forward to and helps you see that light in the distance.

WHEN RESULTS COME OUT: IF YOU PASSED, READ ON HERE. IF YOU WILL BE RE-TAKING THE EXAM, READ THE NEXT CHAPTER

You can live with whatever results arrive when you know you gave it your all. *You owe it to yourself to leave the exam able to honestly say, "I did my best."*

If you passed, which I very much hope you did (!), then you will have powerful proof that you will be able to pass the bar exam. If you did not pass this time, you will need to pull every ounce of confidence together to learn from this experience and train for success on the next administration.

Be especially kind to yourself just before the results come out. Waiting for results is often horribly stressful. Go see a funny movie. Take an afternoon off for a hike or walk. Have a bubble bath and champagne. Distract yourself with positives. You are smart and worthy, regardless of this one test result. Surround yourself with good and positive people who will love and support you no matter what.

If you are a friend or family member of someone awaiting results, be even more kind. Dredge up every ounce of respect and compassion you can find. Back off, and wait to see what that person wants from you. Give them space. Provide comfort and laughter for when that is called. Be a positive distraction. Realize that even if your loved one is not expressing it, they are consumed with waiting for the exam results, one way or another.

PLAN YOUR NEXT GOALS

After you find out you passed, think about what is next. That might be graduating from law school. It might be a law-related part-time job. It might be some other opportunity that is only available in your school after you pass this exam. Whatever it is, always be working toward the next goal.

Again, I am certainly hoping you passed the first time around, but if you did not, follow the strategies in the next chapter and be sure to pass the next time.

CHAPTER 9

RE-TAKING THE EXAM

"There are no secrets to success. It is the result of preparation, hard work, and learning from failure."

—COLIN POWELL—

IF YOU DID NOT PASS

If you did not pass, you must focus forward on passing next time. After you have given yourself time to feel disappointment, you will want to diagnosis reasons you did not pass and prepare to pass next time.

Do any of these reasons people commonly fail the exam fit your situation?

1. You were not worried enough.

You got by in 1L. You thought you would knock it out on FYLSX, *It can't be that tough*, you thought. But it was.

Solution:

If the exam was harder than you expected, you need to train more rigorously this time. This exam is a different ballgame from law school, physically and mentally. In law school, each final exam covered one subject alone; the FYLSX cover three subjects at the same time, all of which require you to memorize and quickly recall many rules.

2. You were too worried.

You were filled with so much anxiety that you could not relax enough to learn the material. You couldn't absorb the rules because you were completely stressed.

Solution:

This time, plan to sleep more, take more breaks, and do more physical exercise. You cannot study effectively for twenty hours a day, and you don't need to in order to pass. Just be diligent and disciplined and use every day as productively as possible.

3. **You did not really learn the law.**

You did not know enough law. You may even have memorized rules but didn't understand them and therefore did not know how to effectively apply them under the time pressure.

Solution:

Accept this, and hit the books. You *will* learn the rules this time. If you don't understand the explanation of a certain concept in one source, try another. As a lawyer, if you did not understand the client's problem, would you wing it? No. You would find a way to learn what you need to know (or refer the case out if you must).

4. **You learned law, but you did not train by completing practice tests under timed conditions.**

Imagine an out-of-shape person wanting to be fit reading dozens of books on fitness and watching fitness videos but not exercising.

Solution:

Go beyond reading and watching videos; complete the practice tests so you are ready to perform!

5. **You were "The Dreamer."**

You went beyond the scope of MCQs, reading things into fact patterns that weren't there. You assumed facts not in evidence.

Solution:

The graders craft exam questions precisely. So, next time, read slowly and carefully. Stay away from "what ifs." Analyze the facts they give you. Use those facts and only those facts along with the rules you have learned to reason to the best answer choices.

6. You have weak reading comprehension skills.

You really don't understand what you are reading. Either you are nervous, trying to read too fast, or have not developed your reading skills thoroughly enough.

Solution:

The FYLSX, like all standardized tests, is largely a test of reading comprehension. Reading is the success thread that runs through every MCQ. Yes, you must know the law very well. But even when you know every rule (and every exception to every rule), your reading skills must also be in top shape to pass. Work on reading and self-assessing. Read aloud and touch each word as you read. Complete many practice tests and study the explanatory answers for every answer choice to see where your reading is not careful or precise enough. (If you have time and want a good exercise, try reading and summarizing, in one to three sentences, all the articles in the opinion section of the newspaper or a news blog each day—this will develop your comprehension skills and keep you informed at the same time!) Last, seek trustworthy help if your reading weakness is due to English being a second language.

7. You are a practicing professional in another field and resent this test.

You are licensed as a professional in another field. You are in law school. You shouldn't be asked to take this test.

Solution:

Don't waste time resenting the exam. Focus on passing it and on all the good you will be able to do with your law license, for yourself and others.

8. You were uncomfortable with the testing conditions.

You may have been unfamiliar with the testing or proctoring software and this might have thrown you.

Solution:

Read all the information from the State bar, over and over to be sure you understand it all. Next, practice as much as possible with exam software and in the location where you will take and under the conditions you will take the exam.

9. You didn't manage time well enough.

Time ran away without you. You were caught with moments to go and unanswered or barely answered questions.

Solution:

Even one question left unanswered can be problematic depending on how many you missed. Practice a lot, and under timed conditions. Have a plan to guess if you run out of time.

10. If none of those reasons fits your situation, maybe you were simply unlucky.

Some people do just have a bad day or bad luck. If so, your solution is simple: Dust yourself off and get back to work. Pass the next exam!

A Look Back in Time

Take a moment now and jot down some things you did on your previous exam that you now see hurt you.

WHAT WILL YOU DO DIFFERENTLY

Now, turn to what you will do differently next time. Re-read passages in earlier chapters and transfer points that resonated into a success plan for your next exam.

Note several things you did not do last time and are committed to doing next time:

____

____

____

____

____

____

Now, update your Success Plan (from Chapter 2). Or, write one if you never drafted a Success Plan for the last exam.

FYLSX Success Target Date:

I ***will pass*** the FYLSX on

____

Signed— *[date]*

FYLSX Registration:

I have completed all application and registration requirements. ☐ Yes ☐ Not yet

This time, I will use the following FYLSX Study Resources:

Last time I used:

____

This time I am using:

___ Adaptibar

___ West *Step-by-Step Guides*

___ Other

My Dedicated FYLSX Time:

Last time I dedicated ___ hours per week to FYLSX exam study. Next time I will devote __ hours per week, starting on ____________.

Last time I worked while I was studying. This time I have requested at least some time off to focus on my FYLSX studies. ☐ Yes ☐ No

Last time I did not manage distractions as well as I need to. This time I will find a way to manage or defer the following:

My biggest distractions tend to be:

Written FYLSX Study Schedule:

Last time I did not have a written study schedule. This time I am creating one: ☐ Yes ☐ No

Last time I studied in a place that was not effective (or where I was too frequently interrupted). This time, I have I identified the following as places I can study effectively, without interruption (e.g., office, home, law library):

Last time people interrupted me a lot. This time I have informed people in my inner circle about my study schedule so they know when I cannot be interrupted. ☐ Yes ☐ Not yet

Last time my study schedule was vague (or I didn't have one.) This time, my study schedule includes hours for specific tasks, such as:

- Actively reading and studying *Step-by-Step Guides* (or other outlines) _____
- Creating my own summary outlines (personalized "cheat sheets") _____
- Memorizing the law _____
- Completing MCQs under timed conditions and studying explanatory answers _____

Confidence and Motivation:

I know my confidence took a hit because of not passing. I am working on acknowledging that I still have many strengths that I know will assist in passing the next exam including:

1. ____

2. ____

3. ____

At this point, I still need to focus on improving the following challenges:

1. ____

2. ____

3. ____

Other FYLSX Exam Planning Issues:

Health issues:

I have taken steps to deal with any health issues that might interfere with my ability to do my best on the exam. ☐ Yes ☐ No

I received accommodations in law school and expect to receive the same or similar accommodations on the exam and have thus completed all the necessary paperwork to apply for such accommodations. ☐ Yes ☐ No

I have had my vision and hearing checked in the past year. ☐ Yes ☐ No

Dependent care:

I have taken steps to arrange for any needed care for children, older or ill relatives, pets, etc. ☐ Yes ☐ No

I hope that completing this sort of a success plan will carry you forward. It's an age old saying, but sometimes slow and steady really does win the race! Keep confident and work steadily toward passing the next time!!

Conclusion

Hopefully, you now see the Baby Bar as something challenging but totally doable.

Seeing the news that you passed will bring an incomparable high. Making it across this first "finish line," gives you the confidence you need to go on, graduate from law school, pass the bar exam, and enjoy a thriving career.

Remember these strategies for success whenever you embark on a new challenge. Carry the positive mindset message of this book with you.

Above all know that you have what it takes, and you *are* a success!